# A LOOK AT LATIN AMERICAN LIFESTYLES

SIL MUSEUM OF ANTHROPOLOGY

PUBLICATION 2

William R. Merrifield
*Museum Director*

Irvine Davis
*Academic Publications Coordinator*

# A LOOK
# AT
# LATIN AMERICAN
# LIFESTYLES

*by*
MARVIN K. MAYERS

SIL MUSEUM OF ANTHROPOLOGY
Dallas, Texas
1976

© Summer Institute of Linguistics, Inc. 1976

Cover design by Ted Smith, Jr.

*Library of Congress Catalog Card Number: 76-18494*
*ISBN 0-88312-151-4*

*This title available at*
Summer Institute of Linguistics, Huntington Beach, CA 92648

# Contents

|  | Introduction | 1 |
|---|---|---|
| CHAPTER 1 | First Impressions | 4 |
| 2 | Multisociety | 13 |
| 3 | Status | 21 |
| 4 | The Behavior of Status | 29 |
| 5 | Manliness and Female Honor | 37 |
| 6 | Marriage | 43 |
| 7 | The Family | 50 |
| 8 | Extensions of the Family | 55 |
| 9 | The Church | 60 |
| 10 | The Military | 69 |
| 11 | Government | 74 |
| 12 | The Woman | 80 |
| 13 | Activities | 84 |
| 14 | Values | 90 |
| 15 | The Economic Life | 98 |
| 16 | The Changing Scene in Latin America | 106 |
| 17 | The Agent of Change | 112 |
|  | Bibliography | 118 |

# *Introduction*

Ask a North American what words come to his mind when the word Latin is mentioned. He may respond with lazy, easy-going, spontaneous, non-aggressive, flirtatious, dishonest, religious, festive, fatalistic, bullfight enthusiast, member of large families, volatile, personable, generous, hospitable. He does not intend these to be derogatory, but rather descriptive.

Ask a Latin American what words come to mind when North American is mentioned. He may respond in much the same way, though with a totally different list of words—aggressive, loud-mouthed, brutally frank, optimistic, casual, pragmatic, independent, materialistic, monied, organized, impersonal, idealistic, rich, dumb, snobbish, tourist-minded, clock watchers, often called Yankee. He will disclaim, just as the North American, any sense of placing a value judgment. This is the way they are; one must put up with it.

Such perceptions of another people affect all of one's associations with these people. Certainly the two lifestyles differ. That is no particular problem. The problem is that each takes the differences of the other personally—almost as a personal affront with the result that each group tries to make over the other. If this does not work, each group regards the other as dumb, slow or stupid.

There is a far better way to interact and that is through mutual understanding within an atmosphere of trust. Many people have suggested this, but much of the "understanding" has been a grasp of facts about the two societies—their gross national product, their population size, details of political operation.

True understanding can come only in terms of interpersonal relationships. What brings two people or groups together in ways that will develop mutual confidence? What are the keys to decision making? How does one influence another without the other feeling manipulated? How do friendships grow and develop? What is it about a person that another can admire?

# A LOOK AT LATIN AMERICAN LIFESTYLES

The answers to these questions and many more come from understanding the behavior of people within differing relationships. The average person from outside a particular society is totally unaware of these behavior patterns which have carefully defined expectations cued for correct response. The cueing systems in two respective societies differ and frequently clash, resulting in tension. Tensions and conflict form a poor foundation for effective interpersonal relations.

There are procedures that help those entering another society to be more sensitive to the expectations of that culture, though not guaranteed to always reduce tension.

*Mutual respect* is called the "helping relationship" by Carl Rodgers. Reciprocal relationships develop when each accepts and knows the other as he accepts and knows himself. Neither puts undue strain on the other to change and each can be a whole man in his own lifestyle. Each can do, think, or say that which is at least respected, though not necessarily believed or taken over by the other.

Each can accept the other as he is. This is not the end result but the beginning of change. With this solid beginning, each can adapt to the other with a minimum of tension for each will feel he is a totally valid person in the eyes of the other. Acceptance helps build one's self respect as well as respect for another. In a climate of respect, adaptation to another lifestyle becomes easier.

*Awareness of difference* becomes the immediate result of mutual respect for each is looking at the other rather than at himself. He becomes aware of the tastes, desires and interests of the other rather than of his own. He begins to compare the two systems in which each operates, objectifying his own, comparing it with the other. Through this comparative study of cultures he becomes enriched as his own lifestyle expands and as he develops the flexibility to leave and reenter his own without stress.

*Bridges of rapport* can be built when tensions develop and requirements for resolving differences can be recognized. The compliment, the explanation, the show of interest, the apology that is verbal or that requires action are some of the ways of building bridges between peoples of differing cultures. The intent of one person may be to cut down the other, to show his superiority over the other, or to bring some reflection of evil on the other. These attitudes and responses alienate and produce a chasm in relationships that prevent each from having any beneficial effect on the other.

In interpersonal relationships, the excitement comes when each person is developing in keeping with his own uniqueness. There is nothing more deadening to a person than to be pressured by another to reject or modify his own distinctive lifestyle to conform to another's lifestyle, especially when that person has no desire to be "made over". This pressure enslaves rather than frees, however good the original intent may have been. The Latin American, even as the North American, is worthy of freedom to develop in keeping with that which makes him Latin. His life, within his own culture, can be totally fulfilled and his contribution to world interests can be tremendous.

I wish to acknowledge especially my wife's contributions to this volume for she and I encountered the Latin American together and found our previous biases changing together from those of suspicion to those of love and respect. Many of the ideas have been sharpened as we have discussed them together. This has also been true in relation to my student friends at Wheaton College. It was not until I began teaching the course on Latin American Peoples that my various experiences and insights gained in Central America fell together into recognizable patterns. My students pressed me to extend my insights, as much as was possible, to other areas of Latin America so that the material might be more widely applicable. Where it is not applicable, I can only say, I didn't push it far enough. Perhaps the one discovering such will choose to produce a companion volume to pick up such patterns and expressions.

I also wish to express my appreciation to the Summer Institute of Linguistics under whose auspices I spent the better part of thirteen years in Latin America. And I am grateful for the help of Mrs. Vendla Walton who rewrote some sections, adding clarity. The Organization of American States provided me with special research funds to write my doctoral thesis on the Mayan Indian people, but many of my insights for this material came as I encountered the Indian with the Latin culture and my knowledge of both Indian and Latin cultures has developed equally.

The volume to follow is designed to develop respect for other cultures, increase an awareness of cultural differences and recognize ways of insuring rapport between cultures while keeping each intact.

# Chapter 1

# First Impressions

My wife and I entered Latin America to live in Guatemala. We had our first child within the first months of our residence. Some friends in the States sent us a little skirt for our baby girl and in a few days we received notice from customs that the skirt had arrived. I first went to the local post office but was directed to the airport since the package had come airmail. At the airport the officials informed me I would have to work through an agent of the customs office in order to receive the package. It was not possible to have it handed to me over the counter. I was directed to the waiting room where I would find the agent.

As I entered the waiting room, a number of thoughts ran through my mind: I would find a man in uniform who would be neat and courteous. I would probably have to wait a day or so. It might cost me a dollar but would be worth it.

Much to my surprise, I found awaiting me a grubby, tattered, unshaven, pleasant but withdrawn, chain-smoking man with fingers coated with nicotine. I was distressed and disgusted. Must I work through him?

He informed me that the process of getting the package through customs would take a week. A week later I went back but the agent was nowhere to be found. The second time I tried, I found him but the package was not available. He informed me I would have to wait another week. I waited and again had difficulty making contact with him. Finally we got together. The package would cost six dollars. I was stunned and showed my displeasure by shouting at him. Finally, I paid the bill and received the package, noting that the customs office had marked the little orlon skirt "silk", which accounted for the enormous charge.

One day my wife and I accompanied some friends to the market place.

Our friends saw something they liked and proceeded to bargain with the salesgirl for the item. She suggested a price. They offered half of that price. The girl rejected that offer and countered with another. Finally, after about five minutes of bargaining, a price was settled upon and my friends left with their purchase. I was chagrined and confused. Is this the way we will have to proceed, I asked myself. Will we have to do this for each item we purchase? I felt it would be cheating the salespeople.

Another time, our family was invited to accompany a Latin family on a picnic. According to our own traditional way, we prepared a few sandwiches (two for each member of the family), included some fruit, beverage, and a dessert and were on our way. We met our friends at the appointed time and place and received a shock. The picnic we had imagined was more like a family reunion. Members of the immediate family were there, as were relatives with their children, a few other friends, housemaids to prepare the food, and farmhands to clean the field where the picnic was to be held. Preparations had begun early that morning when the hands were sent to clean the field and carry out tables and chairs (not the folding variety). The women and their housegirls were already busy preparing the food—chicken, pork, cakes and pastrys, both hot and cold beverages, and other specialities too numerous to mention. We were observing total mobilization and were embarrassed with our little bag of sandwiches.

We moved into the highland area of Guatemala and began to look around for someone to help us learn the Indian language of the area. We found one promising young man who appeared to have the abilities that would make him a good language helper. However, he was hesitant to work for us since we could not offer him steady work. He didn't want to work for even one week since he had this tremendous sense of needing a *patrón* and being hired for a year or for his lifetime.

We received a windfall and were able to purchase a house rather than rent one. As far as we had been concerned, the psychology of renting involved putting nothing into the house that couldn't be taken with us when we moved. We began wanting our own place that we could fix up with permanent improvements. We found a house—at least part of a house, and decided it would be quite adequate without too much remodelling. So we tried to purchase it. However, as we looked for the owner, we were literally unable to talk with him. We were always able to find out where he was—at least where he was thought to be, but when we arrived at that location, we would find that he had departed for his other property, or the city or somewhere else. We did find a man who indicated that he could arrange things for us. Naturally we distrusted this approach, feeling that were we to talk to the owner directly we could get

## A LOOK AT LATIN AMERICAN LIFESTYLES

the best deal on the house and not have to pay extra because he had an agent. So we kept trying to locate the owner and our frustration continued to grow. Finally, we left it in the hands of his friend and within a month we had made a deal, arranged for the proper legal papers and proceeded to put the house into shape for occupancy.

When we entered Guatemala, we carried with us a few appliances such as an iron and an electric coffeepot which would likely need attention sometime during our stay there. Sure enough, one of them went bad and we needed the help of a repairman. After inquiring of our friends we discovered there was a capable serviceman located on a particular street in the heart of town. We went to that street and began to look for his shop. Again we had certain expectations of the type of shop it would be. We would enter a glass front door and walk into an area where there would be a counter with new and old appliances, some for sale and some for repair. Behind would be a partition separating the sales area from the shop and warehouse area. We saw a number of such storefronts but none that appeared to do any business in appliances. Instead we discovered a shallow stall, open to the street, with a counter that was certainly well worn, with the most ancient appliances on display that we had ever seen. I wondered how the place was locked up at night. I'm sure it was but the process must have been intriguing. Remembering that my friends had indicated that this was the best repairman in the city, I took courage and approached the counter. He assured me he could fix the appliance and that I would have it back within a week at best. Naturally, I was there on the day appointed for my wife made use of the appliance frequently and I did not want her to be without it. It was not ready and I was informed it would most certainly be ready the next week, which it was.

We owned a car while we were living in Guatemala, but gasoline was from ten to twenty cents more per gallon than it was in the States at that time. We had to be frugal so frequently took the bus which was much cheaper. We could ride completely around the city for five cents. People would fill the bus at times and we would be as crowded as in a New York or a Tokyo subway. The impression we always received was one of warm bodies. Naturally you would say, what do you expect? But this was an experience I had never had before. Always before there had been some sense of body coolness rather than heat. The Latins seem to be more tactile than North Americans and the warmth of their feeling towards others comes through in this and similar settings.

There was a fine doctor in the state capital near our town whom we consulted from time to time. It was reputed that another doctor took out a patient's gall bladder for every illness. We soon found out that our own doctor always prescribed "rice water" whenever there was a stomach ailment. Through him we learned a great deal about natural medicines and changed our opinion of his being like the gall bladder doctor, especially when his natural and less expensive medicines worked better than the imported medicines. And today these medicines have wider acceptance in the States. Our respect for our rice-water doctor grew through the years. But imagine our chagrin, when he was in the States on vacation, and he was requested to leave a southern restaurant because of his darker skin color. He returned and was walking by our small apartment which we kept in the state capital for shopping trips and which we had loaned to two of our colleagues till their own house was ready for occupancy. The apartment had no plumbing so a very simple arrangement had been worked out. A basin was placed on a table by the dutch door, looking out onto the street, and when there was water to dispose of one could toss it out into the street. One of these young ladies using the apartment did just that as our doctor friend was going by. He was irate, seeing this as one more evidence of prejudice.

His trust in us was only restored later when we had moved into an Indian style house on the main highway to Guatemala City. He was driving his jeep back from the city and seeing us in our new home, stopped out of curiosity. He got out of his car, walked by us brusquely, entered the house without saying a word and proceeded to look about him. He saw a mud daub wall house with corn leaf roof, dirt floors, mats as ceilings and simple pine furniture. He left as abruptly as he came, but we heard from friends that he was so impressed with our simple living conditions that he had no more rancor over the prejudice of Americans and we discovered in later contacts that our old relationship prevailed. Much later his words were conveyed to us, "If Americans can come and live in that kind of house, I will never say anything against Americans again."

While we were living in that house, my wife had a birthday. I wired the store where we shopped at the state capital, requesting that they send a gift via the bus that made daily trips to Guatemala City. The trip took about thirteen hours at that time so the bus left the state capital quite early. The morning of the delivery, my family was deep in sleep when the bus arrived and the driver blew his air horn directly outside our shuttered window. It was so raw and startling that our children began crying. I drew on my trousers as quickly as possible and went out to meet the driver, but still the delay was enough for them to blow the air horn again. With all of this it quickly turned into a gala event and the bus passengers were enjoying our discomposure. Finally the arrangements were completed and the bus left for the city, but not before putting into the mind of the driver a very delightful idea. Whenever he or his associates would round the turn of the highway leading past our house, they would lay on the air horn and picture again our adverse response so early in the morning, hours before our normal time for arising.

Such impressions leave one in states of embarrassment, of irritation, of surprise, of shock. In the earliest stages of contact with a different culture the different ways of life intrigue; later on these same ways disturb. They leave one with not only a distaste for the people of this other culture; they also leave one with a feeling of distrust. And the distrust is quite easily reciprocated.

## The attitude changers

Our interest in Guatemala was to help the Pocomchi Indian people. To do this we needed to learn their language and lifestyle. The Spanish people played no part in this grand plan; in fact, they were seen as a liability in accomplishing it. Therefore, every experience arousing irritation with the Latin was made even worse as we saw them in this sense of liability. They couldn't win as far as we were concerned. They had two strikes against them.

This all began to change when a Latin woman knocked at our door and asked us to teach her English. English appears to be a prestige language in Latin America and many educated persons want to be able to speak at least some English. We put her off explaining that we were not there to teach English, but we finally yielded to her requests and proceeded to spend about an hour a week with her. She would come into town from her farm each Saturday morning for market and after making her purchases she would come to our home for her lesson. We were not there to teach English nor were we there to have such association with the Latins and the irritation continued to intensify, until one day we began to realize something very special was happening. As we, in our stumbling way, proceeded to teach her English, she was teaching us her lifeway and we were beginning to tune in to a tremendous social system, and getting to know some very beautiful people within that system. We saw qualities of life that had never been talked about in our presence before, qualities that we have not seen in people of any other cultures.

Through our Latin friend, we began to know her husband. He was a second generation Latin, his father having been a German who married a Latin woman. He was also a hard drinker and when drinking, his whole complexion turned a bright red and his eyes were terribly bloodshot. When a lesser man would be flat on his back, he would still be going strong. He was the owner of a coffee farm and had dozens of farmhands working for him. He was a hard taskmaster, a fact the Indian men did not like, but he was fair and just and this made up for the former trait of demanding hard work. They also liked to work for him because he fulfilled his responsibilities as an overlord—something that not all farm owners did. In every sense, he cared for his people and would often be in their huts caring for a sick person or taking someone in special need to the state capital.

As we got to know this man, we found him an avid hunter and he would frequently bring us venison. At first the hand was extended in handshake but then the arm went out and we were caught in the traditional Latin *abrazo* or hug of greeting. One day, after not having seen these friends for months, we passed on a highway and we both applied brakes and got out to greet one another. Never have we been caught in such an intense hug—an indication of the deepest, most intense feeling for the other person. We were elated to have friends such as these.

With the beginning of our change of attitude toward the Latin, other experiences could now reinforce the good impressions rather than the bad. These same people opened up numerous good experiences that we remember with great pleasure. We were visiting in their home over a Christmas holiday. When we arrived we encountered their nephew, another doctor serving in the state capital. We had had previous contact with him and our greeting was most cordial. He and his wife had apparently been there a few days and were to stay during our visit, as well.

That evening we went off to bed and found ourselves in a large, handsomely decorated bedroom. In the morning, arising at an early hour conditioned into me by my contact with the Indian people, I walked to the front of the house and was standing on the corner of the large cement slab used for drying coffee beans. The sunrise was magnificent and I was enjoying myself enormously when I caught sight of our friend the doctor leaving the coffee shed in his nightclothes. Just a little surprised, I greeted him and asked how he had spent the night. He responded that he had had an excellent sleep. My curiosity was great and I asked him where he had slept. He responded that he had slept on the coffee beans. By way of further explanation, he assured me that they made a soft bed—perhaps more comfortable than a regular bed. I then discovered that he and his wife had had the bedroom now provided for us, but that they had chosen to give it up on our coming, and take the coffee bin bed. We were startled and thoroughly shaken to think that anyone would give up a lovely bedroom to strangers and sleep in the shed. It was even more incomprehensible, at the time, since doctors have the very highest standing in the community and that he would so humble himself for us was beyond imagination.

**The discovery process**

There is the tendency to see people of another society as just people. If we get along with them then we reason that they have a similar personality to ours. If we like the things they do we tend to respond to them as fine people. First impressions are important to the one entering another society since they have such a definitive part to play in whether the response to the new is positive or negative. Once our attitude changed, from bad to good, we began to discover all kinds of exciting things about the people of Latin America and their lifeways.

Each of the incidents I have mentioned was a step in the process of understanding the Latin culture—a step in changing our attitudes from negative to positive.

We discovered that there were formal agents of customs with offices, secretaries, desks and more North American type arrangements. Yet, even after I began using these seemingly more responsible agents, when I had an especially tough deal, I turned it over to the very first agent I had encountered—the shabby, nicotine-stained free lance agent. He could really take care of the tough deal.

I discovered bargaining to be a most exciting experience, and one that revealed the "mettle" of the man. The peoples' respect and confidence in me grew as I developed tough, though fair bargaining practices. They accepted me as one of their own, and through this means, I received some of my earliest signs of acceptance into the community.

The picnic helped us realize the tremendous importance of the family—not only the nuclear family but the relatives as well. Had we not tumbled to this early, I'm quite sure our contact and influence among them would have been seriously limited. The picnic is in effect a family reunion and treated in this way gives one an opportunity to see in one place the people your friends deem of great importance.

My worker's refusal to help us because of his need to have a *patrón* or a full time boss, opened to us the intricacies of Latin-Indian affairs. We were there for the good of the Indian, but this could never be divorced from the good of the Latin. Without one there could not exist the other. The good of one developed the good of the other. Yet, we discovered that it was more one of role distinction than of race. The Indian was oriented to the land producing and the Latin to what was produced and role distinction developed meaningfully in keeping with these different orientations.

The problem we had buying our house from the original owner and the expectations of our working through a go-between or intermediary alerted us to this intricate practice of gaining favorable decisions. We found it difficult at times, if not impossible, to work through someone rather than by face-to-face encounter. However, we found that the intermediary-arranged decisions were usually the most favorable, and the most satisfying.

The bus experiences and those with our doctor friend opened up to us some of the personal matters of lifestyle and the problems of cross-cultural contact. The North American tends to be prejudiced against people that are so much more warm, outgoing and tactile than they themselves are. Deep down, they feel that physical persuaders rather than mental and logical ones are being used. The Latin tends to be prejudiced toward those who appear of higher status, with more power. It is assumed that they will quite naturally take advantage of the situation.

Our encounters with our farm host and hostess and their nephew revealed to us the significance of the status system in Latin society—the sense of English being a prestige language, and the willingness for an already high status person to yield to someone perceived to be of higher status yet.

In the succeeding chapters of this orientation manual to the Latin lifeway, we will probe further in these various areas of culture and lifestyle to better understand the intricacies of the Latin social structure and its expression. Principles will be provided to better understand the Latin American with a Spanish heritage. Each sector of Latin society applies these principles in its own unique way. Some principles will not apply to certain sectors of Latin society. The reader is encouraged to apply these principles as guides to more effective interpersonal relationships, not as rules which always apply in every setting.

Separate volumes need to be written on each sector of Latin life as well as on those areas with Portuguese or English language and culture sources. Perhaps this book will become the inspiration for such additional resources.

## For further reading

Alexander, Robert J., *Today's Latin America,* Doubleday and Company, Inc., N.Y., 1962.
Ellis, Joseph A., *Latin America, Its Peoples and Institutions,* The Bruce Publishing Company, N.Y., 1971.
Fals-Borda, Orlando, *Peasant Society in the Colombian Andes,* University of Florida Press, Gainesville, 1962.
Freyre, Gilberto, *The Masters and the Slaves,* Alfred A. Knopf, N.Y., 1964.
Gillin, John, *Moche, A Peruvian Coastal Community,* U.S. Government Printing Office, Washington, D.C., 1947.
Lewis, Oscar, *The Children of Sanchez,* Vintage Books, Random House, N.Y., 1961.
Radler, D.H., *El Gringo, The Yankee Image in Latin America,* Chilton Company, Phila., 1962.
Redfield, Robert, *Tepoztlan, A Mexican Village,* University of Chicago Press, Chicago, 1942.
Reichel-Dolmatoff, G. and A., *The People of Aritama,* University of Chicago Press, Chicago, 1961.

## A LOOK AT LATIN AMERICAN LIFESTYLES

Richardson, Miles, *San Pedro, Colombia,* Holt, Rinehart and Winston, N.Y., 1970.
Rivera, Julius, *Latin America, A Sociocultural Interpretation,* Appleton, Century and Crofts, N.Y., 1971.
de Ulloa, Jorge Juan and Antonio, *A Voyage to South America,* Alfred A. Knopf, N.Y., 1964.
Wagley, Charles, *Amazon Town,* MacMillan Company, N.Y., 1953.
Wolf, Eric R., and Edward C. Hansen, *The Human Condition in Latin America,* Oxford University Press, London, 1972.

## Chapter 2

## Multisociety

When one first enters another society and begins tuning into their distinctive culture, individual impressions and fleeting glimpses give the feeling that there is more to this experience than one had first thought, that there are bits and pieces of something that might be part of a larger whole. Slowly, patterns of language and of culture form and the visitor gets the feeling of order and arrangement. The parts form into patterns—both similar and different than those in the source society of the visitor. It is only much later that the pattern forming is recognized to be again only partial and pertaining to a given zone, a specific community, or to one person. The parts forming into wholes form ever larger patterns of wholes with each whole giving completeness to a larger, more complex whole.

The concept suggested by pattern and complexity of larger pattern has been named the "systems approach". Management has used it to good effect in business organization and production (Churchman 1968). British social anthropologists have been applying this approach to the study of society for many years.

Latin society is a total system that has both differences and similarities to North American society. The various components of the system vary from one sociogeographic area to another but are integral parts of this whole; from one sociopolitical zone to another but are again integral parts of this whole. Each area, where Spanish language and culture have taken hold, forms distinctive patterns but are recognizable as of Spanish origin. Such is true of Spain, of Spanish background Latin America and of the Philippines (Mayers 1970). This also is true of each nation in Latin America, with distinctions of food, dress, social organization, and sound and lexical differences within the language. Finally, within each community, there is variation of speech, dress, thought and belief.

The components of the system involve matters of kinship, of reciprocal responsibility, of status, of church practice, of political behavior and of economic relations. Whereas family name (and marriage to gain a certain family name), insures upward social mobility within the status system, education is a more immediate means of upward mobility in the Philippines. Within one community, the meal pattern will involve three meals a day, much on the order of certain North American subcultures, but a community directly across the river will involve a four meal a day pattern. Breakfast will be small and at the time of arising while the "coffee break" time at ten in the morning will be a full meal. Lunch will be served after one and dinner around seven in the evening.

The typical North American is untrained to see a whole system and how the various components of the system work together within the whole. Such was the case when advisors entered certain Latin nations and recommended the levying of a nationwide income tax. Each Latin nation already has a national income tax which centers in the extended family, rather than it being part of the monolithic national levy as in the United States. The head of each extended family or equivalent family pays, out of his pocket, for all or most of the services and responsibilities handled by our national government. These involve health, education, protection, welfare, etc. When a national levy is made, the head of the extended family is then forced to pay twice for the same services. Generally, in the United States, local, state and national taxes go for different services. Whenever they do not, there is a hue and cry. It is this effect that comes about when a so-called national tax is introduced into Latin American countries.

## The multiplicity of cultural expression

Latin (Spanish) America is distinct in many ways from Spain, and from other Spanish background nations such as the Philippines. There are the phenotypic distinctions of darker skin and Indian type body features. There are linguistic differences running from sound changes (e.g. the retroflexed "s" used in place of the trilled "r", and the "dz" sound replacing the "ll" or "y" sound of Spanish) through to changes of grammar and lexicon, (e.g. *coche* used variously for pig and automobile). There are also distinctions of dress, living styles, beliefs, etc. that give one clear identity as a Latin.

Each nation within Latin America is quite distinct. Linguistic differences provide some of the lesser distinctions. People in Guatemala tend to be rural and provincial in outlook whereas those in Venezuela tend to be urban. South Americans tend to have more "church" awareness whereas those in Central America are less tied to the church and more narrowly religious. In Central America the strength of the extended family is quite noticeable even to the thoroughgoing political control of Salvador by a few families, whereas in South America this extreme focus on the extended family is moderated. In some more urban areas it is almost lost.

Within Latin American society, taken as a socioeconomic whole, numerous distinctions of subculture can be made. Charles Wagley has differentiated nine separate types or subcultures existing throughout Latin America (Wagley and Harris). These are not to be taken as absolute in any sense, rather descriptive within a taxonomy that permits flexibility in application and a non-judgmental response to difference.

1. Tribal Indian (aboriginal peoples):

    Tribes made up of villages or bands united only by a common language and customs and the conscious need to form a "people" against all outsiders.

    Tribes (often villages or bands of the same tribe) at war with one another.

    Power of the chief seldom extends beyond one or more village or band.

    Homes in lowland areas.

2. Modern Indian types:

    Homes in highland areas.

    Organized into native states.

    Integrated into colonial societies by forms of forced labor.

    Have produced a kind of folk society.

    Have European type settlements and government.

    Many may be bilingual, work in mines on *fincas,* etc.

    Are mainly horticulturalists raising native American crops.

    Community is the landholding unit.

    Loyalty is local rather than national.

    Each community is endagomous.

3. Peasant types (*mestizos* in Mexico, *ladinos* in Guatemala, *cholos* in Peru, *caboclos, tabareus, caipiras, matutes* in Brazil):

    Similar in many respects to modern Indian.

    Generally horticulturalists using slash and burn techniques to grow maize, manioc and potatoes.

    Have archaic European patterns.

# A LOOK AT LATIN AMERICAN LIFESTYLES

    Have national loyalty.

    Use markets.

    Speak national tongue (except in Haiti where a Creole is spoken).

    Have literacy, play soccer, celebrate holidays, recognize national heroes, dress city style.

    Lead a slower-paced life than town people.

4. Engenho (*ingenio* in Spanish):

    Have privately owned and operated plantations of sugar cane and coffee.

    Have patriarchal group, caste society, closely knit groups.

    Capital more important than land.

    Have an intimacy and mutual dependence between workers and employers.

5. Usina plantation:

    Have larger, less intimate, centralized commercial farms.

    Are a rural proletariat.

    Characterized by Mintz in 1953.

6. Town:

    Have fairs, religious centers, regional markets.

    Some are farming, manual-laboring people.

    Others are non-farming, landlords, white-collar workers, bureaucratic, own businesses.

    Control most of the political and economic power in the community.

    Have radios, receive mail, send children away to school, have servants.

    Catholicism is more orthodox.

7. Metropolitan upper class:

    Disdain for manual labor.

8. Metropolitan middle class:

    Admiration for courtly manners.

9. Urban proletariat types:

    Love of luxury.

    Careful separation of role in each sex.

There is also a culture of poverty (Lewis 1968) existing in Latin America as defined by Oscar Lewis.

> As an anthropologist I have tried to understand poverty and its associated traits as a culture or, more accurately, as a subculture with its own structure and rationale—a way of life passed down from generation to generation. This view directs attention to the fact that the culture of poverty in modern nations is not only a matter of economic deprivation, of disorganization, or of the absence of something. It is also something positive and provides some rewards without which the poor could hardly carry on.

This culture of poverty is more pronounced in some nations, e.g. Mexico, and in some areas in each nation, e.g. zones of displaced rural and Indian peoples such as slum areas or areas taken over by Indian background people who have been forced, for some reason, to leave their land.

Besides these more pronounced differences, there are local and provincial differences that are frequently as subtle as the direction of the firewood when it is being carried home (up one's back or across it), or the amount of flowers in the patio, or the degree of help the husband will give his wife.

Within Latin society are members of other societies, as well, such as Chinese, Japanese, Germans, Scandinavians, all living as Latins with no immediate tie to their homeland.

## Tuning into system

One of the things I noted upon entering the Latin American household was that the first people we were meeting were relatives of our newly made friends. We first met a sister, then a brother, then the neighbors across the street, then the parents and then other relatives. As we met each one, we were made aware of their relationship to our friends: this is my husband's oldest brother, or this is my mother's brother's daughter. We realized also that we met each in relation to some domain within the house. The brother and sister we met in the living and dining room area. The parents came from a part of the house we had originally seen being used only by the host and his immediate family.

This pattern of encounter and reinforcement through language and behavior is very significant for Spanish background societies. The family is an important element of Spanish life; not the nuclear family as in North America but the extended family. The extended family in its totality involves the nuclear family, blood and affinal relatives, ritual relatives (the neighbors were part of the family through this extension of the family), and maids, houseboys, and pets.

I was visiting a local pastor in the community and while talking with him in a restaurant, a judge and two of his associates walked in. I was immediately introduced to the judge but not to his associates. They did not appear to be upset and I overlooked what to me was a slight. In some way, the pastor in sizing up the situation saw the judge and me as worthy of being introduced but saw his employees and me as unworthy of being introduced. I considered a number of alternatives set up by the situation and came to the conclusion that there was some type of stratification operating that placed the judge and me on one rank level and the employees on some other level. It was only later, after further observation and inquiry, that I was able to establish it as the characteristic Spanish strata-rank system operating with everyone either above or below everyone else in rank. I had seen this operating in terms of the space behavior in the household, i.e. higher status people, in relation to the hosts, had unlimited access to the house and lower status persons had less access to the house. All further involvement in Latin America confirmed this type of stratification system.

I was to discover that the strata-rank system operating in Latin America had very much the same composition and implications to behavior as the relationship existing in North American society between teacher and pupil, employer and employee or parent and child. One is of higher status in relation to the other. The difference between North American and Latin American involvement, however, is that the North American has the interpersonal relational system in "pockets", while the Spanish background societies extend throughout the entire society.

The average person entering another society looks first for the exotic, the strange, the different. This is especially true of the tourist who returns with exciting tales or pictures of the extraordinary. Some tourists plan their trips so that they can take in all the exotica available for that particular area. Unfortunately, those going into another society frequently wind up looking for this kind of thing and overlook significant aspects of the culture that would help them carry out their business more effectively. Too many early missionaries fell into the trap of exotica and wound up missing significant opportunities for service.

Another thing that the average person, entering another culture or subculture, sees first is that which is distasteful to him. Such a reaction can quickly condition one's attitude toward the people who have such customs and lifeways. Their response in turn will be a distrust of those who do not like the way they live and do things.

Such approaches to another culture leave the visitor reacting positively when he sees something strange, negatively when he sees something he doesn't like. It is quite possible that his entire stay in the host country can turn out much like a pendulum swinging from one extreme of appreciation to another of distaste. What is overlooked is what a person is actually like; how he really lives; how he makes decisions and places values on people; things and activities; and how he organizes people and things.

The things you hear first are bound to be significant. Hearing the relationship of the first people I met to the host revealed the great importance of the extended family. Places to which I was taken indicated the historical sites known to the people and told me something of their loyalty in relation to the activities that made that site important. The behavior of people in relation to your behavior opens up further insight as to system. The fact that the pastor introduced me to the judge and not his employees told me something significant that would serve as the key to relationships of people within the society.

The behavior of people in relation to others of their own culture opens up other insights of significance. Children subject to others besides their own blood parents open up strands of loyalty and responsibility beyond the nuclear family. Division of labor that incorporates members of an extended family as distinct from members of another extended family begins to define the lines of the primary group within the society. When there are special events such as births or funerals or weddings, indication is made of groupings and membership of groupings, and of respect-prestige relationships existing within the community. If only family members attend the funeral of the child, but all members of a community attend the funeral of an adult one gets clues to the extension of the family and to stratification within the community. Tuning into the perceived responsibilities of a given leader indicate whether the society places certain obligations such as the education of children in the hands of the family or the state.

Tuning into the system operating within the society is not difficult, but it takes special training for those who have never had objective contact with a second culture or subculture. It does require one's lifetime to become truly bilingual, i.e. fluent in the language of origin as well as the language of the host community; bicultural, i.e. able to cope with all the challenges and experiences of the culture or origin as well as that of the host; and finally, bitrustable, i.e. able to establish an effective trust bond or trust relationship within one's own associations as well as within the contact setting (Rodgers 1961).

The chapters to follow will serve as further guidelines to permit the reader to tune more effectively into the system of society operating in Latin America.

## For further reading

Churchman, C. West, *The Systems Approach,* Dell Publishing Company, N.Y., 1968.

# A LOOK AT LATIN AMERICAN LIFESTYLES

Heath, Dwight B. and Richard N. Adams, *Contemporary Cultures and Societies in Latin America,* Random House, N.Y., 1965.

Lewis, Oscar, "The Culture of Poverty", in Yehudi A. Cohen, *Man in Adaptation: Cultural Present,* Aldine, Chicago, 1968.

Mayers, Marvin K., *Notes on Christian Outreach in the Philippines,* William Carey Library, Pasadena, 1970.

Redfield, Robert, *Folk Culture of Yucatan,* University of Chicago Press, Chicago, 1941.

Rogers, Carl, *On Being a Person,* Houghton Mifflin, Boston, 1961.

Schurz, William L., *This New World,* E. P. Dutton Company, N.Y., 1964.

Wagley, Charles and Marvin Harris, *Minorities in the New World, Six Case Studies,* Columbia University Press, N.Y., 1958.

Wolf, Eric, "Types of Latin American Peasantry", in Yehudi A. Cohen, *Man in Adaptation: Cultural Present,* Aldine, Chicago, 1968.

# Chapter 3

# *Status*

Max Weber distinguished three types of stratified systems operating within society: 1) economic, referring to possession of goods and opportunities for income; 2) status, based on social estimations of honor; and 3) power. The first produces social classes or groups within society whose members hold a number of distinctive statuses in common and who, through the operation of the roles associated with these statuses, develop an awareness of their like interests as against the unlike traits and interests of other groups. North American society utilizes a class type stratified system and its members divide into three primary classes of upper, middle and lower, and perceive, for distinct purposes up to three divisions of each of these, again indicating these internal distinctions as upper, middle and lower, e.g. the upper middle class.

The second type of stratified system produces strata-rank distinctions. Perhaps the best metaphor to utilize in discussing such a system is the "ladder". Every person or every group perceives itself on a distinct rung of the status ladder, and is ranked in terms of one position on the ladder in relation to all others on the ladder. Latin American society utilizes such a strata-rank system with the primary reference point being the individual. Each individual is on a distinct rung of the status ladder in relation to everyone else. The family and regularly associating members of a given family may be perceived as having the same status as the individual.

North American society, though having the class system as its primary means of relating its members, also has certain settings in which a status-rank system operates. This secondary system operates within the teacher-student relationship allowing the teacher to teach the student. Both can be members of the same class though one stands in a respect relation to the other that forces certain demands upon the other, e.g. the student cannot talk back to the teacher. It also operates within the parent-child relationship to allow the parents to complete the early socialization of the child within the class system. Otherwise, the child might never learn from the parents and there would have to be some other system established to give one the right to tell the other what to do.

In much the same way, Latin America has the two systems operating within the larger society with the two aspects of stratification reversed. The primary system operating is that of strata-rank calling for just about every operation in the society to be ranked, e.g. persons, cities, means of transportation, etc. The secondary system is that of class. Throughout the entire society there is what might be called a "shadow" class system operating—useful in terms of reference, e.g. the upper classes; but also operational in the emerging urban life where the strata-rank distinctions are much too limiting in larger population areas and developing industrial complexes.

## The social machinery of status

There are four basic social mechanisms of strata-rank: 1) everyone wants to associate with the person above him in status, but he does not want to associate with those below him; 2) influence can only extend down the status ladder since in a real sense it is impossible to influence one with whom you have no contact; 3) in order to influence someone above your level of status, it is necessary to arrange with someone of higher status to influence him, i.e. an intermediary; and 4) you tend to trust someone seeking to influence you if he is nearer your own status level and conversely to distrust one who is too far above your level.

In a system of strata-rank it is natural for someone to seek to raise his status. The higher he can get, the better off he is. One of the primary means of rising on the status ladder is through others who are higher on the ladder than oneself. Therefore, it would certainly be a waste to associate with lower status people when association with higher status people may mean rising in standing in the community. Because of this, means of social mobility (see below) will be prominent in dealings with others and it will be necessary to establish, as quickly as possible, the place of the other person in relation to oneself. The first questions which are asked of another person reflect this need to know just where he stands. These questions involve family, place of birth, occupation (not for the purpose of knowing income as in North America, but in order to know one's standing as reflected in employment.) When one associates with those of lower rank than oneself, he may be perceived as being at a lower level. If one does associate with lower status people for a time, he needs to return regularly to his higher status associations to maintain his highest level and to guarantee that his lower status associations are seen in the context of the purpose of those associations. Any group or organization operating within the Latin American community needs to have in its top positions those who have high status and who maintain it through appropriate behavior. For example, a North American operation will be perceived to be of the highest status and its leaders potential for high status. Therefore someone in the organization needs to play golf regularly or exhibit visibly some other form of high status behavior so that no question could arise as to the standing of the organization.

Since one can influence only those whom he directly contacts the tendency is for influence patterns to develop down rather than up the ladder. Two significant implications arise from such a process. One's influence potential is pegged to one's rank allowing one to influence all those below him and none of those above him (without other means of extending influence), and anyone of lower status is susceptible to the influence of everyone above him. Many North Americans entering Latin America are middle class people and are content to be seen as middle class by the Latin. Without realizing it, therefore the North American limits his influence and establishes organizations that are middle status in the perception of those dealing with them. The North American, only later, realizes that his customers or clients are rather uninfluential insofar as the total society is concerned and they have a deep seated distrust of the product since few upper status people seem to trust the product. Apparently, this limits the outreach of the Protestant church in Latin America. The church is seen as of middle status since its founders were apparently willing to exhibit only middle status behavior. Thus the upper status people within the society remain relatively untouched by the church, with a few notable exceptions, as when a North American pastors a Latin church, or degreed professionals staff a service institution of education or medicine.

Simply because one is lower status than another does not hinder influence if the appropriate connections have been made prior to the time of influence. Such connections provide one with intermediaries or go-betweens who are in some way responsible to the lower status person to such a degree that they are willing, in fact consider it their duty, to influence the person or group so named. The problem that confronts a given person in Latin America, is how to get high status people associated with them and thus indebted to them for such a purpose.

Spanish background society has handled this through the experience of the life crisis. There are, generally speaking, four principal life crises recognized in society: birth, puberty, marriage, and death. Of these four,

## A LOOK AT LATIN AMERICAN LIFESTYLES

two have become the primary foci of family extension (see Chapter 8). At the birth of a child or at the marriage of a child, godparents are selected to serve as co-parents. In some areas of strong Catholic dominance, godparents will also be selected at puberty, during a ceremony called "confirmation". At each occasion, the parents of the child make careful selection from among their friends and acquaintances as to whom they would like to bring into their family "as if they were in reality family". They will most likely choose some person or couple of higher status than themselves, and someone of equal status. It is a high honor to be thus selected. The person named as godparent must have some very strong reason to refuse. Otherwise both the family naming them and the community would think of them with displeasure. It is through this association, that a person, when he needs to influence someone of higher status, will make plans utilizing one of even higher status. He considers each of the godparents aligned with his family and selects that one whom he feels will have the best chance of gaining his desired goals. He will then approach the one so selected and proceed to convince him that influence is needed. In the process, new indebtedness will form, this time on the part of the one making the request. Such indebtedness will be "paid off" during the continued association of the godparents.

The intermediary is free to approach the problem in any way he deems best. If the person seeking the influence made a wise choice, there is very little question as to the result. The request is likely to be granted. In case the person has chosen unwisely, or there are extenuating circumstances, the request will not be granted. This will in no way reflect on the intermediary, though generally he will regret not having been able to serve. The relationship returns, then, to the pre-request stage and the one seeking influence will begin again to plan his strategy, making use of the same or a different intermediary depending upon how he sees the situation at this time. He seldom is thwarted to the degree that he will entirely abandon his plan of influence.

Someone of considerably higher rank than the one being contacted is immediately distrusted by the one so contacted. Later, after observing the higher status person over a period of time, the distrust may turn to trust.

### Social mobility

Social mobility appears to be one of the chief concerns of the Latin American. This is not a concern that is like the "keeping up with the Joneses" pattern of the North American. Rather, it is a built-in drive of the system. To fulfill oneself as a Latin is not necessarily for selfish reasons. A person will take every opportunity to rise in status. There are three primary opportunities presented to the Latin: marriage, accumulation of wealth and education. Accumulation of wealth does not include bonus wealth (e.g. winning lottery money) which is something distributed to family.

In Latin America, the sense of national identity comes from association with, and combination of, extended families. This is in sharp contrast to the North American whose sense of national identity comes from individual involvement within the "bulk" or corporate entity "nation". Therefore, in Latin America, the sense of family identity, or the symbol of family, is the family name. The family name thus becomes important, not only during the period of one's life but also during the period of the life of the family. Any means of perpetuating the family name is of primary importance. Anything that results in the termination of family name is looked upon as a tragedy to be avoided at all costs. This is part of the need each Latin has to have a son, for it is through the male line that the family is perpetuated. This can also begin to explain the deep emotional involvement the Latin man has both with his own son, and also with his grandson. Further, the family name is well established in relation to a given level of status. Having a family name permits one the rights of a given status and gives him the opportunity to not only learn the behavior of that status, but also to exhibit it in the community.

Marriage provides the only social mechanism in Latin society for the change of name and as such becomes a primary means of rising in status. If someone marries into a higher status family, he is entitled to the privilege of that family and thus the privilege of that status. Mothers are aware of the best marriage opportunities for their children and will quite aggressively proceed to set things up. One family went miles to visit a farm owned by people of higher status than themselves in order to arrange a marriage between their daughter and the son of the higher status people. This was in spite of the fact that the farm was near to bankruptcy, which the aggressive family must have known. This period of visitation lasted for months though previously there had been only occasional contact. Following this intensive period of visitation there was little continued contact.

At marriage, a bargain is struck that equalizes the arrangement, granting to the lower status family the potential for the higher status of the other family and giving, in some way, the higher status family repayment for the privilege of the higher status. This can involve money, a gift of house or land, or of services extended.

Wealth is generally associated with family. Those of higher status have more wealth than those of lower status, or at least the ability to lay their hands on wealth. The family-wealth correlation has been sustained by some families but lost by others. Some family names are associated with wealth that no longer exists. These people have a difficult time coming up with sufficient funds to meet the normal demands of their social existence, such as gifts at weddings. Yet, they are careful to meet these expectations to maintain the image of their higher status.

Anyone able to "come into" wealth by legitimate means such as investments, increase of salary, some development that has come from new training or new use of old abilities, becomes eligible for a rise in status. Any money, such as a windfall, winning a lottery, getting a bonus payment at work, etc., does not necessarily entitle one to rise in status. Such money is expected to be given to the members of one's extended family as there is need, given to the church, or in some way distributed for the gain of others. Occasionally some can be invested, but the rise in status does not attend the initial investment, but rather the expenditure of the gain in keeping with status expectations.

Education becomes important in social mobility because of the potential for greater wealth that comes from a higher paying job or by developed abilities. Education overseas provides even greater opportunity for upward mobility. Unfortunately, this also provides a route out of the source country permanently. The student leaves the country and intends to get those credentials that will entitle him to higher status. He becomes involved in the host country through job opportunity or marriage and may even acquire a "taste" for that different way of life.

Upward mobility is part of the system of stratification enabling people to relate effectively to others. Everyone therefore strives to improve his standing. The reverse is also true. Since someone rising presents a threat to those above, others are trying to prevent someone else from rising. The tension from rising and its counter resistance—prevention from rising—produces much of the uniqueness of Latin social relations. This tension also produces an emerging middle class in large population areas where the strain can only be reduced by letting more than one person or family be perceived as being on a given level.

## Assignment of rank

For the majority of Latins, the assignment of rank in the strata-rank system is made through time as family adjusts to family in keeping with the means for social mobility as well as the expression of one's status. When there is a change of some kind such as someone moving into a community, or a member of a given community that has married or been educated returns, there is a period of adjustment that continues until all parties have resolved the status distinctions among them. This new alignment continues until there is a further move on the part of an individual or family.

The priest is a-status in that he is above the status system and is only assigned status in relation to his assignment. He will always be the highest status person within a given church-community. As he moves up within the church hierarchy, by appointment or by being assigned to higher status churches, his status rises. If he were to be assigned below his status level, he would naturally be the highest status person. His vows of celibacy keep him from becoming part of the system operating in the larger society in that he is no longer associated with a given family name. He is set apart to the church by his own family and thus not responsible for the perpetuation of the family, and unable to marry and become associated with the family name of a wife.

The North American comes into the status system at a very high level. Not all outsiders have this privilege but the North American does and can use it to good effect in fulfilling his goals. As he lives up to or fails to live up to the expectations of his high level of status he can maintain it or drop in status. He generally drops because he lives in keeping with the class demands instilled in him in his source society and these are, generally speaking, behaviors of statuses lower than the highest to which he is entitled. Peace Corps men often carried out their dating according to the North American practice which involved public display of affection. Such public display of handholding and kissing is seen as lower status behavior among most Latins causing the North Americans to be lowered in the perception of the people. Missionaries frequently come from the middle class and find it "natural" to exhibit middle class behavior. This causes them to be perceived as middle status rather than higher status and they find themselves virtually unable to reach the upper status members of Latin society.

## Caste

Within any given stratified system of society, the means for moving from one social level to another may be provided and encouraged or withheld and restricted. The latter tends to be the case in Latin America, whenever the Spanish and Indian cultures come into contact. Speaking of the system as it is operating in Guatemala, Tumin suggests that no Ladino (the name given to Spanish background peoples), no matter how humble or denigrated his position, is ever considered by the other Ladinos as socially equal to or below any Indian. Put conversely, no Indian is ever considered by Ladinos to be the social equal or superior of any Ladino no matter how many of the criteria of distinction he may possess. He further states that "Indians exclude Ladinos because they feel them to be a very different kind of people, whereas Ladinos exclude Indians from their social ladders because they think them both different

# A LOOK AT LATIN AMERICAN LIFESTYLES

and inferior." (Tumin 1952). This attitude excludes Indians from Ladino involvement and Ladinos from Indian involvement. In effect then, there is minimum opportunity for Indians to move into the Ladino social circles, except, perhaps, over a number of generations.

Such restriction in social mobility produces two castes: the Spanish background caste and the Indian caste. The two remain basically separated, have as few dealings as possible, and if there are altruistic members within the Spanish background group who suggest that Indians are equal in every way or ought to be, their actions belie their words.

Such a caste system is not inherently evil. It can function quite effectively to give each social group involved an effective and adequate identity as well as social freedom within the parameters of that identity. This has worked quite well insofar as the Spanish background person is concerned in Latin America. It has worked less well among the Indian people who have not been given, nor been permitted to develop those operations which could let them fulfill themselves as Indians.

## For further reading

de Jesús, María, *Child of the Dark,* New American Library, E. P. Dutton Company, N.Y., 1962.

Goldschmidt, Walter and Harry Hoijer, eds., *The Social Anthropology of Latin America,* University of California, Los Angeles, 1970.

Tumin, Melvin, *Caste in a Peasant Society,* Princeton University Press, N.J., 1952.

# Chapter 4

# The Behavior of Status

Upon entering a typical Catholic church in Latin America during some service that has brought the community together, it gradually becomes evident that some distinctions are made in the seating arrangement. The most obvious pattern emerging is that the Spanish background people sit toward the front and the Indian people sit or stand toward the back. With churches having only a few pews, the people using them are generally well dressed, sit back fully into the bench, follow along with the various demands of the service, appear to be reading the appropriate material and will likely greet the priest upon leaving. In churches with more pews, those sitting toward the front will express this pattern of behavior. Farther back will be those who are not as well dressed, seem to have difficulty reading or following when someone is reading, and may only sit on the seat part of the bench rather than lean back. They are likely to leave the church by side doors, or bypass the priest while he is talking with others.

Closer observation will reveal that the better dressed are wearing whole shoes, and the men might even have on imported shoes. Whatever the source, however, they would be kept highly polished. Other men would be wearing less costly brands of shoes, probably only those made in the country itself, and they would be in various stages of wear and polish. There would be other men with leather sandals and still others wearing sandals of car tire rubber with straps of innertube rubber. There would also be the Indians who wore no shoes.

The men sitting toward the front would be wearing clean white shirts and tightly knotted ties. Near them but not with them would be those with soiled white shirts—white nonetheless—and the ties would not be knotted so tightly. Beyond them would be men with white shirts perhaps,

## A LOOK AT LATIN AMERICAN LIFESTYLES

or some faded color, but with no ties. Others would have no white shirt, or a patched shirt, and no tie. If he were asked if he wished to wear a tie, the man of Spanish background would respond, yes, he would wear one if he had one. The Indian would reply, no, what's the point.

If one were a North American, as the service terminated, one would be introduced, most likely, to those with the white shirts, carefully knotted tie, dark suit and shined shoes. One would not likely be introduced to those with soiled shirts, loosely knotted ties and unshined shoes unless the host, himself, were dressed that way.

Where one sits in a public service, what one wears on his feet, how one dresses for given occasions, to whom one is introduced, or not introduced, does not depend on wealth alone. Rather it is a correlation of wealth with family background and the visible evidence for the status accorded to that specific display of wealth in keeping with family. In other words, one lives in keeping with the demands and expectations of one's status level and in turn makes demands on others in keeping with these expectations. How one acts in keeping with his status within the community is termed behavior of status.

Having been introduced to different members of the community, in keeping with their status and their perception of one's status in relation to theirs, it is possible to follow them further into their everyday lives. The better dressed and perceptually higher level people would be bosses, administrators, leaders of unions, or other. Clerks, subordinates and salesmen would be next, day laborers, next, marketeers and small businesses next and then permanently hired hands or *mozos*.

The better dressed and higher status people would be owners and rentors of land. Next would be farmers owning extensive land, then small plot landowners as farmers, non-owners renting small or large land to make their living, non-owners as *mozos* and finally non-owners as squatters.

The higher status people would live in nicer homes in better areas of the community—if not in the center. They would purchase their food from commissaries or supermarkets. They would eat meat regularly, purchasing the better cuts, and would have a more North American diet. Lower status people would live in successively smaller homes down to one of simply four walls and a window in progressively less desirable neighborhoods until the *barranco* or slum area is reached. There the walls will be of cardboard or adobe set on end (making a thin wall and relatively unstable), and the houses literally tied to the steep walls of the cliff side. The people in the nicer homes will shop in the market, or in a local store. Those who live in street front rooms will shop in a storefront in their block and go daily to buy the things they need. Their diets will be marginal and meat will rarely be served, at least not the better cuts. From this point down the status ladder, no cuts of meat will be available, the choice involving only meat with bone or meat without bone.

The patterns of behavior noted above are quite strictly adhered to and each status level knows what they want to eat and wear and the occupations they are to engage in. They also know and sense the restrictions on them and in a variety of ways can discuss consistent and responsible behavior or inconsistent and irresponsible behavior in keeping with a given status level.

Whenever there is a mixing of pattern, such as a person wearing a new white shirt with a dirty tie and shoes, there will be some question as to how he got that and what is his right to wear it. North Americans come under very careful scrutiny in this way since they obviously have money, have cars or access to cars, etc. However, the average North American does not quite maintain himself in keeping with the expectations of the higher status Latins and very quickly appears inconsistent and therefore irresponsible. The North American does not keep his shoes shined as much as his potential status level demands. Nor does he wipe off his car every day or have a man to do that. He does not have a sufficient number of maids in his household. Such inconsistencies of behavior, not living up to all the expectations of his status level, cause the Latin to perceive him at a lower level than he might otherwise be and frequently at a level low enough to keep him from influencing those people he really wishes to influence.

Each nation of Latin America, along with each community within a given nation, has its own list and combination of expectations. An exhaustive list would be both impossible and unnecessary to form. Alerted to the possibilities of status behavior, one can enter a given area and quickly observe the distinctions. It is possible to take someone of equivalent status and inquire as to the primary expectations. It is always wise to continue the observation process since there is some change from year to year and from situation to situation and no one person can completely clue in another to the complexity of social involvement.

It is not necessary to try to live up to all the expectations of the social, religious, political and economic realms but it is important to live up to significant ones and reveal to the community your wisdom. North Americans disregarding any expectations or doing something right merely by chance are considered stupid by the Latins.

## The festival and status behavior

There are many activities and celebrations that give significant clues to the status system operating in a community, and to the behavior called for. Most important of all, these activities give indication of the status of the person with whom you are dealing. The festival and the festival procession are key indicators of status level once the pattern of behavior is worked out.

There are certain festivals that are characteristically Latin. More Latins are likely to participate in the procession, even though the Indian will participate as well within an Indian area. Corpus Cristi is one such processional festival. There are other festivals in which only the Indian population will participate.

Each sociogeographical area in Latin America has its own variation of festival procession behavior but one pattern is as follows:

Lower status Indian men will lead the procession with banners or staffs of authority visible.
Lower status Indian women will bring up the rear of the procession, carrying babies or leading children.
Lower status Latins—both men and women—will walk alongside the procession, primarily in the area of the platform carrying the saint.
Higher status women will follow along directly behind the platform carrying the saint, dressed in their Sunday best and unaccompanied by children.
Higher status men will precede the platform but follow the priest who will be protected from the sun by a canopy held aloft by higher status young men.
Men of varying statuses will carry the platform for a block or two, yielding to other men who have paid an acceptable fee entitling them to this privilege.

A second type of procession, which in a sense is "festival", is the procession of the funeral. Again, status relationships are revealed by examining those participating. Children being taken for burial will attract only the members of their own extended family. As one moves up in age he attracts successively more. The higher status one has as an adult, the more people he will have at his funeral and in the funeral procession. Again, placement reveals the higher and lower status persons. The higher one is closer to the immediate family grouped around the coffin. The lower one is peripheral to the family grouping.

## Neighborhood and status behavior

The neighborhood one lives in is both an indicator of and a control on behavior. All neighborhoods are ranked as to status in relation to all other neighborhoods. If the "right" person enters, there will be a period of adjustment as each individual and family reevaluates its status rank in relation to the newcomer, but the move will be minimally disruptive. If, however, the "wrong" person (someone too high or too low in status) moves in, it is maximally disruptive until the perceived status level of the newcomer is determined by each family and individual, as well as the status level of the newcomer's associates.

If someone of too high a status moves in, the lower status people in the vicinity will operate as beggars or as thieves in a basically unconscious attempt to lower the status of the newcomer. Even if they do not participate in such activities themselves, they will do very little to hinder them. They might indicate their disapproval but they will question not the thief, or the beggar but rather the person who has moved into a neighborhood below his own status.

If someone of too low a status moves in, the higher status people in the vicinity will exhibit embarrassment. They will not like to be seen with or near the newcomers. They will communicate directly or indirectly their status and their desire to live up to their status level. There may even be pressure brought to bear on higher status relatives of the family encouraging them to move.

The North American is expected to move into the highest status communities and when he doesn't he suffers what to him are great indignities at the hands of the neighbors. Very few North Americans are able to merge comfortably within a community in Latin America because of this.

Any given Latin community has either covert or overt means of indicating status areas. If a specific community or city chooses overt means such as numbering, the members of that area will know the relative rank of each part of the larger community and will behave in keeping with that rank. For example, Guatemala City, Guatemala, Central America is divided into zones. These zones are numbered from one to fifteen, fifteen being the latest zone opened up in relation to one which was the very heart of the city and thus the first zone. The zones form in somewhat of a spiral design out from zone one with the last zones formed on the periphery of the spiral. I will call them "zones of compatibility" for that is precisely what they are in relation to each other. Those on a given status level feel compatible with those near them in status. They will not associate with the neighbors to the same degree as will members of a class system of stratification, i.e. socioeconomic as in the case of North America; but they will nonetheless feel more comfortable with these people in their neighborhood than they will if the status distinction is too great. The chart on the following page indicates the status zone pattern of Guatemala City. Numbers indicate the zone and letters represent rela-

# Zones of Acceptability

*Guatemala City*

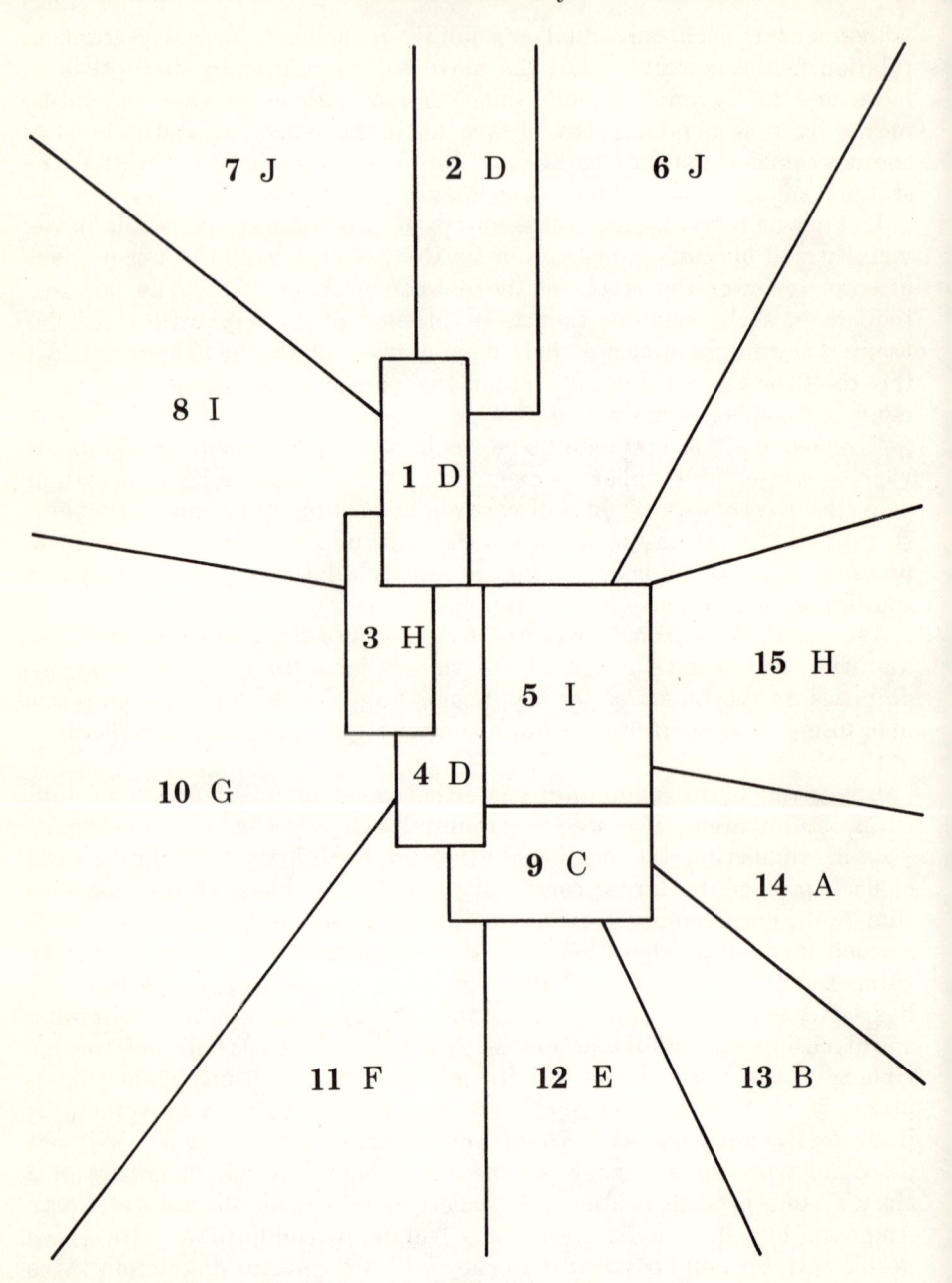

7 J
2 D
6 J
8 I
1 D
3 H
15 H
5 I
10 G
4 D
9 C
14 A
11 F
12 E
13 B

34

tive rank of status in relation to other zones from A, highest status to J, lowest status.

The development of slum communities or low status neighborhoods progresses quite distinctly from those of North America. In North America, the poorer replace the richer. In Latin America the poorer live together in one non-desirable locale resulting in a "shanty town" complex. Often this is a swamp area, or a cliff, *barranco,* or gulch area. Whereas in North America the poorer families usually take over better houses and let them deteriorate, in Latin America people frequently come from rural areas with little or no means of self support leaving rural homes that were more clean, sanitary and durable than the new homes they encounter or construct. Thus the housing is definitely substandard from the start in Latin America whereas it is standard housing deteriorating to substandard in the North American areas. In North America, one can move out and up depending on his ability, education and effort, whereas in Latin America the people are generally stuck for at least one generation. In North America, people leave their original home to move into a slum area because they have heard there is more money to be gained, greater opportunity to advance and greater independence. Perhaps their rationale works for them, perhaps not. In Latin America people move into the slum areas because they have lost something—homes, land, or possessions. Or there may have been feuding or other disruptive situations.

Another phenomenon that occurs in Latin America is that in the zones where higher status Latins live, there will be expensive homes and mansions existing side by side with shanties. In fact such contrasts are indicators of the very highest status neighborhoods. Any piece of land not occupied or protected are targets for squatters. Because of the laws of Latin American nations, squatters' rights can be established after a given period of time. The landowner wishing to protect his parcel from squatters will look up some low status member of his family (family members are the only ones you can really trust) and establish that family on the land. The owner can always move a family member whereas he cannot always move a squatter. These low status, and likely poor relatives, often jump at the chance to move to such an area for such a purpose. It gives them free rent and may even provide a small income. It also brings them into association with richer people and they can benefit from this through influence, perhaps by getting a better job, a greater opportunity, or serving as guardian for a number of other homes.

## Ranking of society's members as status behavior

Were a North American given a list of members of his own community and asked to rank them from most important to least important, he would have a difficult time. He would resist the activity and equivocate so much it would be difficult to determine what he intended. Were an Indian of Latin America given a list of his Indian peers in his "perceived egalitarian" society where everyone is perceived to be on the same status level as everyone else, he would be unable to do so. Were a North American living in Latin America, or an Indian associating with Latins, or the Latin himself given a list of his peers, he could quickly rank them in strata rank and list their relative statuses. All matters of status are thoroughly known and can be objectified when the Latin is given opportunity to do so. Generally speaking, he lives subjectively within his own society and matters of status are adhered to carefully but they are not conscious behavior on his part. He is simply doing what he has to do to survive in his society.

Until one understands the status system operating in Latin America, discovers the nuances from nation to nation and community to community, and can cope with the challenge of the behavior of the system, he will be frustrated in his efforts to relate to and influence the Latin. Once he does tune into the system, however, the entire society opens to him. Operating correctly and carefully, he can ultimately influence the entire society.

## For further reading

Lewis, Oscar, *Five Families,* John Wiley and Sons, N.Y., 1959, and *Pedro Martinez,* Random House, N.Y., 1964, and *La Vida,* Random House, 1966.

Reichel-Dolmatoff, G. and A., *The People of Aritama,* University of Chicago Press, Chicago, 1961.

# Chapter 5

# Manliness and Female Honor

Julian Pitt-Rivers has discussed the Spanish background people as being "bull" oriented. He is suggesting that these people who have a lifeway embracing the bullfight, derive from this symbol, patterns of behavior that give it its own special uniqueness.

Before examining the implications of such a concept or symbol within Spanish background society, it might help to examine a society with a distinct symbolic orientation, perhaps the "lamb". A society orienting its behavior to the symbol of the lamb might tend to have the following behavioral characteristics: meekness, submissiveness, a need for man, and an overall sense of harmlessness. There might be little sexual symbolism and physical aggressiveness involved. Such a society might stress humility as inherent in the life of goodness. It might teach the "turn the other cheek" philosophy of interpersonal relations.

A society orienting its behavior toward a bull symbol might tend to be aggressive, stress conquest, and rely on the strength of man or beast. There could very readily develop sexual aggressiveness in keeping with the concept of fullness or physical virility. There could be an element of danger interjected in interpersonal relations. Humiliation might have some external source rather than being inherent in the concept of goodness.

The bullfight, in its essence, is a pageant that attends the sacrifice of the bull. The bullfighter in his role of *matador* or "slayer of the bull" becomes the bull. He then assumes the qualities of bullness and is the aggressor in all the affairs of life. In a society oriented to the lamb, a sacrifice of lamb would likely establish the sacrifice as an end in itself, that is a symbolic representation completed within the sacrifice. The sacrifice of the bull is simply a means to an end that the *matador* himself might become the bull. In this way, every man becomes bull with the final thrust of the sword.

Pitt-Rivers puts the significance of the moment of killing the bull in this way, "Clearly, such a conceptual evaluation of sexual virility leads to a certain proclivity to justify manliness literally and moral precepts taught in education tend to be outweighed by the desire for such justification." Starting with the physical, the male aggressiveness extends out into all spheres of life: social, religious, economic and political.

This aspect of what is called "national character" therefore has a significant part to play in Spanish or Latin life. It sets up and controls relationships between the sexes, between leaders and followers, between bosses and employees, between higher status people and lower status people, between parents and children. I will term the behavior pattern that attends the bull symbol, "thrust-humiliation". Just as the bull fighter thrusts with his sword to slay the bull, if he misses and must thrust a second or third time, he in essence humiliates the bull. Such humiliation is reflected in the audience response to the bullfighter. He will become a hero and receive positive response if one thrust achieves his goal. By the second thrust, the audience is beginning to turn against him and by the third he is likely to be openly jeered. This is further reflected in the ceremony of presentation to the bull fighter following the fight. The bullfighter will receive both ears of the bull if the thrust has not produced humiliation. If it has been partially humiliating, only one ear will be presented and if there is no positive response to the fight, no ear will be presented. It is in the presentation of the ears of the bull that the bullfighter himself becomes bull.

The Latin will approach a sexual conquest with great caution. He will drop hints, will establish firm associations, will even openly make proposals, which if responded to positively indicate to him that the way is clear for his conquest. If the woman goes through with the arrangement, the Latin male has thrust and is now content and fulfilled as a man. If, however, the woman was only "playing around" and was not serious about completing the arrangement, the Latin male would be humiliated and would then proceed to retaliate by some form of sanction or violence against the person who so violated him.

The Latin will approach a relationship, other than the sexual, in much the same way. He may wish to name a godparent for his child. He will check everything out quite carefully and finally approach the person or couple he is seeking to name. If the matter is agreed upon readily the Latin is content and fulfilled as a person. If there is a hesitancy, or refusal after the thrust has been made, there will be extremely hurt feelings and some type of retaliation is likely to be made at some future time, if only a breaking of the friendship.

A Latin approaches a line-up at a public office in much the same way. He will examine the line, the people in the line, and then make his decision to go to the end of the line or to go to the front. If he feels he is above the status level of the people in the line, he will go to the front. If, after he has made his thrust, someone yells *cola* or "end of line", the Latin is highly offended and may even pick a fight there on the spot. He has prepared for his thrust very carefully and in being called as to his decision, he is humiliated. He loses a degree of his manliness.

## Manliness

The term *machismo* describes this sense of manliness which if ignored or undermined produces humiliation. *Machismo* refers to the ability to conquer, to effect a conquest. To the degree that a man is able to effect conquest, to reflect the fearlessness that attends conquest, and to reflect such virility, to that degree he is a man. To the degree that he is unable to reflect such manliness, to that degree he is less than a man. Anyone keeping him from this manliness, or from achieving at least the perception of manliness, is considered an enemy, one to be dealt with, if not destroyed.

## Honor and reputation

*Machismo* as concept and practice does not stand alone in Spanish background settings. It is paired with personal honor, the woman's side of the coin. If the male is motivated by conquest, the female is motivated by honor and reputation. Her place in Latin society is defined as upholding such honor and reputation. Any woman who fails to uphold them is considered as *sin vergüenza* or "without honor".

The woman is born with moral rectitude. She has this until her death unless she does something to lose it. Having lost it she is seen as someone with no feeling for either her own reputation or her children's. She is perceived as someone without understanding or sensitivity, as indiscreet, or as blatant. It is therefore vitally important that she maintain her personal honor at all costs. The men in her life make this their life mission. Thus, a father or brother will always provide the daughter-sister with a chaperone to make sure she is not molested in periods of association with the opposite sex. Any possible taint to mother-daughter-sister is covered up, never to be revealed. Any adverse claims on the women in a man's life are causes for challenge. The woman is perceived as pure and this perception must be maintained at all costs.

# A LOOK AT LATIN AMERICAN LIFESTYLES

The woman can lose her personal honor in at least three ways: 1) by committing some sexual act with a male and being found out, 2) by making a point of sexual liaison with or without reason, or 3) by her response to her husband's acts when they become blatant and obvious. In other words, a man or woman can engage in extra-marital liaisons and maintain their reputation (he as manly and she as full of honor) as long as they engage in the liaison with "taste". The moment either shows lack of taste, the woman loses her honor.

Two terms are used to refer to the relationship of man to woman where taste has not been exercised: *cabrón* or "male goat", and *cuco* from cuckoo. The he-goat is the symbol of male sexuality. It refers not to him whose manifestation of that quality is the cause of the trouble, but to him whose implied lack of manliness has allowed the other to replace him, that is "to put horns on him". The cuckoo is a bird who lays its eggs in the nest of another bird. Within the Spanish context, however, there is an inversion. The word, therefore, refers not to him who plays the role of the cuckoo, but to the victim whose role he usurps. Thus there is in reality no so-called "double standard" in Spanish society, so much as a "revelation" standard that affects either male or female. The key seems to be not the one who participates in extra-marital activity, but rather, the one who reveals it and in what context and manner it is revealed. If there is in any sense a double standard, it simply resolves itself in the greater frequency of adverse revelation of the woman's activities than of the man's.

## Taste and lack of taste

A Latin man who had a number of mistresses provided each a piece of property and a house. Further, he gave them the expected provision of a hundred pounds of corn each month along with other food stuffs. He took care of these four women and at his death, they received their land and house as their own. Another man turned one woman out into the street with insufficient means and was condemned by the community for the loss of honor his mistress had achieved. Whereas the first maintained his manliness throughout his life, the latter quickly lost it for not fulfilling his obligation to the woman.

A doctor moved into a community away from the city and his wife refused to accompany him, preferring to stay in the city. He took a woman of that area as his mistress. His wife, hearing of this, went to the town and accused him of infidelity. She warned the other woman that she was to have nothing further to do with her husband. The wife then returned to the city. The man and his mistress continued cohabiting and the community turned against the wife for stirring up trouble. The wife, not the mistress, lost her honor.

A very rich man took a beautiful woman as his mistress. The man was old and kept the woman through lavish monetary and clothing gifts. A younger man came along and won her heart. Because the older man did nothing to get rid of the younger man, the community saw him as the *cuco* who let himself be supplanted.

A young seminarian went to a rural community each weekend to minister. Because his wife was with child, she was unable to accompany him over the rough roads. He lived in the home of the lay leader of the church and the elder's daughter was assigned to keep his room clean. She did a satisfactory job of cleaning but in her every contact with him she questioned and challenged his virility as a man. Finally, in complete frustration, he took her and molested her sexually. Her parents naturally complained to the teachers at the seminary and the boy was expelled from the seminary. The girl was seen as the innocent victim of a sexual assault and no blame was attached to her.

A Protestant missionary driving to the post office each morning in a rural Guatemalan community would pass a neighbor woman with a large basket on her head going to market which was just around the corner from the post office. He also recognized the woman as one attending the local Protestant church. He graciously picked her up each time he encountered her and rumor quickly spread throughout the community that she was becoming his mistress. Some of the respected elders of the church communicated this to him and urged him to cease picking her up even though they never doubted his innocence in the matter.

The Latin man and woman have distinct ways of looking at the world. He looks through the eyes of conquest, and she through the eyes of maintaining her honor and reputation. Both may have sexual liaisons so long as they handle these experiences with taste and not reveal nor let them be revealed. The social controls on behavior are such that the one revealing the liaison becomes the one who loses out. The man loses his perception of manliness and becomes a *cabrón* or *cuco* and the woman loses her personal honor. The social structure is such, however, that the society is oriented to babies which it needs for perpetuation, and to male authority which it needs for law and order, and to the provision of a legitimate role for the unmarried female.

The North American, by watching the Latin American, can learn a great deal about approaching a public office where he wishes to get something done. If he stands in line when the people perceive him as higher status than themselves he will lose respect in their eyes. If he moves to the head of the line unwisely he may be humiliated by the call to return to line. He can examine his own perceived status (from the point of view of the Latin) and if he is of sufficiently high status, he should—in fact, must—go to the head of the line.

He should be careful about any associations with Latin women. Jesting with a maid in the house can be readily misunderstood, both by the maid and by those with whom the maid associates. Having a live-in maid needs to be handled with a great deal of discretion. He should be extremely cautious about accusing a Latin of sexual indiscretion, for fear that he, the accuser, might lose the respect of the people and undo all the good he is seeking to accomplish.

The North American woman can be aware of her need to provide herself with a "chaperone" when moving about the Latin community. A child provides this type of reputation protection beautifully. She needs to be aware of problems of living alone. She needs to effect a modesty of dress and be cautious in talking to males, especially those who are strangers to her.

## For further reading

Aramoni, Aniceto, "Machismo", in Bernard Landis and Edward S. Tauber, *In the Name of Life,* Holt, Rinehart and Winston, Inc., N.Y., 1971.

Nida, Eugene, *Understanding Latin Americans,* William Carey Library, Pasadena, 1974.

Pitt, Rivers, Julian, *The People of the Sierra,* University of Chicago Press, Chicago, 1961.

*Chapter 6*

*Marriage*

Roberto had a wife and added a mistress who happened to be the family maid. The wife became quite upset and demanded that the maid leave. She later discovered that the maid was still the mistress. This upset her tremendously. She made life miserable for Roberto and he began spending more and more time with his mistress. He prepared a house on a piece of land for her which became her home. Finally his wife left him and received a divorce decree severing their relationship permanently.

Since Roberto was now free to marry, the logical thing would be for him to marry his mistress. She refused. She wanted him for herself but did not want to marry him. To marry him would be to lose him. Their relationship continued as before. He spent all of his free time with her. He kept improving the living quarters, something he had not done previously. They did things together such as bathing in the river in a secluded spot on their farm that few married couples ever did. Their personal behavior toward each other was one of "lovers" instead of a married couple.

The case study just referred to does not in any way suggest that marriage is not desired in Latin America. It simply suggests that marriage has certain advantages, but also certain disadvantages.

The man stands to gain quite a bit by marriage. The prestige of a church wedding for him is equivalent to the North American college degree in its potential for opening doors of opportunity and establishing relationships with those who can be of social and economic aid. Further, if he is able to marry up the social ladder, he stands to gain in prestige. If the woman has any private wealth or inheritance, he gains the right to supervise, though not dissipate, the wife's wealth. Since the man is minimally restricted in the physical domain, he can afford to wait in order to strike the most auspicious marriage.

The woman gains a stability that is not present outside of marriage. She can be fulfilled as a woman in all the ways important to her by bearing children within a "good reputation" setting, by gaining new respect within her own family, and by looking forward to a secure future as her children return to her all the prestige and provision provided in their childhood. She knows she is likely to become the strong moral leader of the family and to outlive her husband and thus handle most of the family affairs in her period of greatest maturity. Marriage is also likely to free her from large family responsibilities since the girls are exploited in the family of their source, serving as babysitter, maid, or cook, depending upon the need and the degree of busyness of the mother. Finally, upon marriage, the woman is entitled to physical relations within a legitimate or "good reputation" setting, though she frequently discovers, much to her chagrin, that it may not last long.

The man also stands to lose by marrying. He finds he has less chance with other women and he must be much more discreet. The gain in social standing within his community is offset by his loss of conquest potential and the ability to reveal his total sense of manliness. Not that there are no opportunities. He just has to work harder at the process. Perhaps, more than this even, is the responsibility he has of providing his wife a new home. Prior to marriage, bargains are struck that take some men their entire lifetime to fulfill. The wife is not content, and will not leave her husband in peace until all of the details of such bargains are fulfilled. These details, differentially perceived, often become the source of constant nagging. Such nagging is not part of the mistress experience and this tends to make the mistress relationship pleasant by comparison. Whereas he is not fully responsible for providing adequate living arrangements for his mistress, when he marries, he becomes fully responsible for providing house, land and staples so that his family do not become the wards of the community.

The woman loses many personal rights when she marries. The husband becomes the stated authority within the household. He is responsible for the legal aspects of the social and economic life of the family and thus has the right to supervise her wealth if she has any. He is not entitled to abuse or waste the wealth or inheritance but he has the final word as to its use. Further, she is likely to experience a shift in her husband's thinking from herself to other women. This is what Roberto's mistress was attempting to avoid. Since the value of physical relations lies in the conquest rather than in physical gratification, one conquest releases the male to seek the next conquest. Such shift in thinking is impossible to thwart within the marriage relationship since by definition, the man has full rights over the body of the wife. It is, however, possible to thwart this in the mistress relationship by remaining the mistress, though there is the risk the woman takes that he might tire of her. Besides, if the woman is married, the house and other shared possessions remain in the husband's name; if unmarried these are placed in the wife's name. They then revert to her own family rather than the family of her husband. At times, the family will urge her not to get married so that the gain can be added to her inheritance and thus benefit her family of origin. Finally, she can always leave her man but not her husband.

Though Latin society tends to encourage marriage, there are many forces at work in Latin society that cause the unmarried state to be highly attractive. The North American assumes that marriage will take place, whereas the Latin has more of a choice in such a matter. North American society has begun to have equivalent experiences within certain youth subcultures where marriage may follow a period of living together, or in certain situations within the adult subculture where there are certain advantages attending the single state, such as tax and social security benefits for two singles living together rather than as a married couple.

## When is marriage?

In North American society, marriage tends to be seen as a point in time. They were married at such and such a time and after that time there was no question as to their married state. In Latin society, marriage is seen more as a process. Two are in the process of being married. Thus, from the time that a suitable mate is fixed upon, the marriage process is in operation. This tends to reduce the premarriage period to one of covert seeking out an appropriate mate. The immediate family is involved. The extended family is involved. Negotiations are begun with one family and then these might be dropped. The larger public might be unaware of the negotiations, but not unaware of what was going on.

Engagement becomes a critical point in this process and could, behaviorally, be indicated as the actual point of marriage. At engagement the basic negotiations involving the pair are completed. Each potential mate has committed to the other and the families of each have approved. Following engagement the couple are permitted to be together unchaperoned. Thus, whether there is any sexual liaison or not, the perception of the Latin is that the woman has lost her virginity. She is thus spoiled for any further good marriage in the event this particular contract ultimately falls through. If such an engagement is broken, the girl may remain a spinster, or even commit suicide, rather than attempt

## A LOOK AT LATIN AMERICAN LIFESTYLES

another marriage contract. Men with good reputations, however much they may "love" such a girl, are not likely to marry her.

It is when the couple goes to the city hall that they are, in the eyes of the state, married. At this time they are entitled to all the opportunities and obligations of the married state. It is this experience that becomes binding for the married pair, not the church wedding as in North America. The church wedding will usually follow but it is the signature of the clerk in the city hall, not the attending priest or minister, that is binding on the couple.

There are a number of distinct types of marriage which are legitimate in Latin America. The first of these is the town and church marriage that is legally binding on the pair and for which they need a legal divorce decree to sever. Though this is not what would be called "arranged" marriage in the Far Eastern sense where the families select the mate for the male, still there is a great deal of family involvement in the selection of the mate. The boy or girl will have to think seriously of marrying when the families are opposed to the union. Various sanctions may attend such a choice including loss of inheritance or banishment from the family home.

A second type of legal marriage is that of mutual consent. Two people choose to live together as man and woman without the official paper work of the city hall and the wedding of the church. They may make this choice because of lack of funds or for the gains referred to above. Such a married state is gained through elopement, or by a man taking into his home an abandoned engaged girl with child, It is seen as a legitimate arrangement by the state with specific terminology of *soltero* and *soltera* applied to the condition and laws that protect the participants and the state. The children are called *niños naturales* or "natural children".

Such a married condition can become totally binding on the pair and the families involved through a *de hecho* or "after the fact" decree following a certain legal period after the death of the male. This can also make the mistress relationship binding in the same way following the death of the male and the legal wife.

The third type of legal relationship is that of concubinage, referred to previously as the mistress arrangement. The two are called *querido* and *querida* or "loved one" and are referred to as *en la calle* or "in the street". Again, such an arrangement is potentially legal in the sense that the relationship a woman has with a man can be declared legitimate after the fact.

Such types of married relationships are clearly differentiated from prostitution. The latter is illegitimate in every sense in Latin America, though practiced, whereas the former types are fully legitimate and approved within the larger Latin community. There is, of course, a ranking attached to the order indicated above where the town and church marriage is the most completely legal and fulfilling, but the mutual consent and the mistress arrangements are a vital part of the fabric of Latin life.

## Choice of mate

Even as the North American has certain specific qualities he is looking for in a marriage mate, so does the Latin. These include higher status, family approval, physical appearance, and preparation for that specific marriage.

Perhaps the highest priority evidenced in selection of a mate is status—higher than one's own and higher than that of one's immediate family. This is not something that will appear at the top of the list in family discussion. Rather, it will enter constantly into the conversation and be one of the primary items resulting in negative sanction if it is not heeded. This means that though a person will not overtly admit to such selection based on status, still the status consideration is the most powerfull in determining the selection of mate. Ideally, the mate sought should be of higher status than the one engaged in search. It is not possible for both to find a mate of higher status. This results in a bargain being struck so that the mate of perceived lower status is able to demonstrate his ability to meet the expectations of the family of higher status. There may be a money settlement, a land settlement, a house built or an agreement where any or all will become part of the agreement through time, almost like mortgage payments. Such an arrangement is made not so much for "bride price" or dowry but rather as a status equalizer. Unless it is apparent to those of higher status that the mate can live up to that status, those of higher status stand to lose ground. Since the drive in stratification results in upward mobility, it is obvious that any union that involves loss of standing in the community would be disastrous.

Without family approval, any status gains for the individual are lost to the family. Latin marriage is not designed so much for the pleasure of the pair or for the development of the nuclear family as for the perpetuation of the immediate family and the extended family or at least that group of associating relatives that support and reinforce the social and economic positions of the members. Such perpetuation is important since the primary socialization of the child is carried out through family and continued identity development and security is guaranteed through family. The child is not dominated by such family ties but because of loyalty he wants to do that, and only that, which will help the family develop through time.

Physical appearance is important to the Latin but not of all-consuming importance. Dark hair is preferred over light, plumpness over thinness and a moderately light skin over light or dark. Any combination of genotype that will produce the desired effect in one's children makes a suitable selection. For example, marriage to a Spaniard, besides producing gains status wise, will also lighten dark skin. This therefore is a very advantageous marriage. Marriage to an Indian will result in darker skin besides whatever it will do to the status position, and so is undesirable. Marriage to a Scandinavian blonde is quite worthless since it involves little status advantage and will lighten the hair along with lightening the skin. Marriage to a darker haired German will do little for status position but will lighten the skin without lightening the hair. Thus, this is a neutral choice with some positive considerations, especially if there is wealth in the German background.

Of least consideration are other factors that might benefit the marriage. Just because a person has education is not a key reason for a mate. The education must mean something else besides degree and learning per se. Missionaries, interested in the training of pastors and their selection of well trained mates to support them in the ministry through Christian education programming are chagrined and disappointed when the young seminarian selects a young, untrained, inexperienced bride. She may have come from a higher status family, have his family's approval, have the looks to suit his taste, and the training is something that he wants to do. One of the tragedies of the educational process that finds a young person studying outside his sociogeographical zone and marrying someone encountered there is the lack of ability to return to his own area for service. One's mate will be basically dissatisfied outside that one's own specific area and will likely find it difficult if not impossible to find acceptance by the mate's family. The only thing that saves such marriages from a lifetime of marginality is the ability for one to find a mate from a higher status subculture as happens when Latins study in the United States and marry a North American. Since the North American is potentially of higher status, the young person is usually able to find someone that will meet with the family's approval.

Part of the choice of mate involves an age discrepancy. Men choose to marry between the ages of twenty and thirty-five. They select mates from the thirteen year old bracket to the age of twenty-five. This will not happen in every case, but is an approved age discrepancy for viable marriages.

## For further reading

Lewis, Oscar, *Five Families,* John Wiley and Sons; and *Life in a Mexican Village: Tepoztlan Revisited,* University of Illinois Press, Urbana, 1963.

Lipset, Seymor Martin and A. Solari, *Elites in Latin America,* Oxford University Press, N.Y., 1967.

Mintz, Sidney, and Eric R. Wolf, "An Analysis of Ritual Coparenthood (*Compadrazgo*)" in Eugene A. Hammel and William Simmons, *Man Makes Sense,* Little Brown and Co., 1970.

Willems, Emilio, "The Structure of the Brazilian Family," *Social Forces,* Vol. 31, May 1953.

# Chapter 7

## The Family

**Growing up in a Latin home**

It is impossible to fully describe all the early influences on a child's life through growing up in a home characteristic of the culture. The details of the mosaic are too numerous to indicate. Each home at each strata level in the society is distinct in many ways. Many of the influences are so subtle that it would be impossible to sort out all the involved patterns and crosspatterns.

There are some characteristics of home life, that are unique and quite distinct from North American patterns. These influence behavior of the Latin and need to be known so that the North American can be aware of ways that he might readily offend the Latin. For example, because of the system of conquest and mistress relationships, a given child will go through life not actually knowing who his real father is. Or he may not be sure that the father he considers his own is really his natural father. This is not to say that all children are born of natural fathers outside their home. The percentage of actual ambiguity of parenthood may be small, but the larger cultural perception is one of "I'm not sure deep down inside of me". Therefore, the question, "Who is your father?" is out of place and potential for embarrassment.

In middle to lower status homes, a child is likely to be born at home with the attendance of midwives. The urban setting is changing this practice with the introduction of hospitals, but the semi-rural and rural Latin seldom has access to these due to distance and funds. Thus an ideal of "natural childbirth" is held by the Latin woman. Since the wife is well taken care of by other women, it is likely that the husband has found some reason to be away.

*The Family*

The child born into the average Latin home is seen more as a burden than as a help. The child is needed by the man as a fulfillment of his manliness and by the woman as her evidence of mature womanliness. However, once this is accomplished, the child becomes part of the debit side of the household until, as an older girl, she becomes useful for child care; or as a boy, he is able to contribute to the economic needs of the household. Nonetheless, childbearing is seen as an obligation, whatever the cost, and the woman fulfills her obligations without question. The woman is freed by childbirth, not bound. Attending that birth will always be some kind of bargain, beginning with that struck upon engagement and marriage and progressing to the actual agreement preceding sexual intercourse. The North American gets the wrong idea about such bargaining, however, seeing it as some cheap thing that people do apart from love. Deep and abiding love can be there and the bargaining simply reinforces it.

Feeding a Latin child is no particular problem. The child is fed when it is hungry. This will be done by the mother, a wet nurse or by the eldest daughter. Anyone unable to actually feed the child will attempt to pacify it in some way. The other children will play with the child, the grandmother will place the child to her dry breast, the father will rock the cradle or swing the hammock. The Latin mother is careful about one thing in particular—she will feed the child if it has slept for a long time, even awakening the child to calm her own fear of a possible problem. This is readily arranged, for the child, as a general rule, sleeps with the mother until some time between the ages of one and two years. The weaning process takes place when the next child is born or some time around the age of two. If the child is difficult to wean, something like chile sauce may be spread on the mother's breast. Otherwise the task of feeding will be placed upon others within the household.

The newborn child is seen as innately evil. If he turns out good, this is a clear indication of the parents' success in training him. If, however, he turns out bad, then it is simply the result of his evil birth and is no reflection on the good intentions of the parents. As soon as the child is born, steps are taken so further evil does not attend the child's development. In the lower status homes this may simply be a string tied around the baby's wrist to ward off the "evil eye". In upper status homes this may be something done at baptism, such as paying for a more elaborate ceremony.

Early childhood in a Latin's life is unique in many ways that clearly distinguish it from a typical North American's life. There is a lack of attention paid the child until sometime around the age of twelve. The child's basic needs are met but beyond this he develops in his own good

## A LOOK AT LATIN AMERICAN LIFESTYLES

time and at his own pace. There is a lack of privacy that permits the child to know pretty much everything that is going on about him. Even in the homes of the upper status, a child has much freer access to the parents' rooms than does the North American child. Frequently the child will sleep in the same bed with other siblings and, especially in the lower statuses, clothing will be shared in ways unknown in North America. There is seldom the extreme definition of my bed vs. yours, my clothing vs. yours, my room vs. yours, my spot vs. yours, that is encountered in North American society. Child care may be by mother, grandmother, older sibling, or by a housegirl or maid. Bathing and personal hygiene takes place when convenient. It is not nearly the ritual it has become in North American society. Dirt is not the problem it is in the United States. The runny nose, the dirty pants, the stained fingernails are cared for at the convenience of the household rather than at the convenience of the child.

At the age of puberty, around twelve or thirteen, life begins to change dramatically for the Latin child. Clothing styles will become more adult, hair will be cut for the first time, and the father will begin paying attention to the boy. Medicine that was previously withheld, due to a fatalism that limited medical attention in the infant and young child period, is now administered sparingly. More punishment will be extended in efforts to make the child "shape up"; there is an overt effort at training that was withheld earlier. The girl child will be expected to participate in household chores such as cooking, unless the household has a cook; or cleaning if there is one. Formal training in the church begins and also the preparation for economic activity.

The youngest boy is saved from the activities, sanctions and punishments of this period. He is allowed to continue much as in early childhood. However, at the age of adulthood, sometime around the twenties, or at the time of marriage, he achieves adult status, even as any other male. It is just that the maturing process is realized in a briefer period.

Especially in the lower and middle status homes, resentments are built up that result in the boy wanting to leave the home. The girl would like to, but is unable to leave permanently unless married. She will therefore return whereas the boy may never. Educational or economic opportunities in another geographical area may provide the opportunity for the severance of such relationships. It is this tension, built up within the home, that often causes the contemporary Latin male to seek his fortunes in the urban centers. Men from rural and semi-rural areas may not return home until they can carry with them the signs of financial success.

## Foci of authority in the family

The father is the stated authority in the family. When he has made a decision, he expects that decision to be carried out. Whenever a Latin man is asked about questions of decision making—who is the final authority and such—he very quickly responds that he is. There is no question but what he is the "boss".

The father is away from the household much of the time due to his business activities, his mistress relationships, or his simple choice to be away. When he is away, the woman makes the decisions and even those made previously by the man may be carried out in ways characteristic of the woman. The child seeing this happening in juxtaposition to the "order" or decision of the father quickly begins to realize that the woman is the real authority in the household. She is the ever present mama and as such guides the children in those things pertaining to reputation, both individual and family, social adjustment and education.

Even though the father is responsible for the economic maintenance of the family, due to his absence and non-support, each woman is likely to have her own means of self support. The living room store or the seamstress business are the most popular means of making money. Each can be done in the household without neglect of children and each can be adequate in provision when there is need. Only the woman handles this money.

Such practices insure the woman a key place in the decision making process for she has the ongoing association with those to be influenced, and she has the independence to make her real authority stick.

## The three adult household

The North American household is a two adult household. Even when another adult is in the house, it is expected that the condition of occupancy is a temporary arrangement, and that the extra adult will not participate in the ongoing life of the household. This latter implies that no punishment will be extended to the children. The extra adult will not participate in the decision making process, nor will that person contribute generally to the support of the household.

The Latin American household is a three adult household. The expectation, whether realized in a given case or not, is that the mother of the wife will be living in the house over an extended period of time and participating in the total life of the family. She is permitted to discipline the children, make her point of view in a sitation requiring decision, and even participate equally with her daughter in running the household. If the mother of the wife is not living in, the husband's mother may, or

# A LOOK AT LATIN AMERICAN LIFESTYLES

even one of the grandfathers. It is not unlikely to find more than one extra adult, but at least one extra is welcomed and readily becomes part of the everyday life of the household.

# Chapter 8

# Extensions of the Family

### Household extensions

Extensions of the family occupying the immediate household with the nuclear family include the service staff and pets. The service staff includes people who serve in such roles as maid, cook, houseboy, chauffeur, and the like. Each becomes part of the family in a distinct way, the maid coming closest of all. Each one of the service staff reinforces the status of the family. As the staff increases, the status rises. Higher status families usually have two or three maids; middle status families may have one paid maid or a member of their extended family sharing responsibilities. It might be a girl attending school and working in a relative's home for her expenses. Lower status families may take in some less fortunate person, usually a girl, to work in the home.

### Kin extensions of the family

The nuclear family consisting of the father, mother and their children is the basic social unit in Latin America. Yet, Latin society cannot be fully understood without realizing the powerful influences of the extended family.

Entrance into the nuclear family is by birth or by adoption. The natural born child is received warmly in keeping with the following priorities: first born male is of highest priority, females are acceptable if they are neither first nor last, the last child should be a male. The child is received less warmly if this ranking is not realized. The first born or last born male receive unenviable consideration in Latin society.

The adopted child is received into the home either through obligation of coparenthood or through sympathy for the child or a need of the adopting family. In North America the child is adopted for the sake of the child, so the child won't have to live in an orphanage, so it will have adequate home life, or the couple needs a child to love. In Latin America the child is adopted for the sake of the family. Granted, when a child is received into a home of higher status than the family of origin, he is benefited, but this benefit turns to the advantage of the family since there are expectations of service to the receiving family that are not wholly fulfilled until death. If the child is of equal or lower status than the receiving family, the exploitation of the adopted child or orphan is much more overt.

Nuclear families tend to relate primarily to other families within their extended family rather than to families of friends (note the exception in the case of ritual extension of the family below). In Latin America the close association of relatives within the extended family has no particular name. In the Philippines, this extended family relationship is called the alliance.

Families within the extended family are held together by common loyalty to each other, to their family name and to the relationship they enjoy as distinct to the outsider. The ties of extended family are maintained by the women of the family. It is their responsibility to see that cordial relationships are maintained within the extended family and that obligations are met in a consistent and acceptable way.

Not all of one's relatives are ever a part of the extended family, even though they can claim the right by blood. The term, extended family, used here refers to the associating relatives. Those that do not associate, due to geographical or social distance, are seen as relatives but no effort is expended in maintaining the cordiality of relations that is true of closer relatives. Those of lower status may be called upon for such activities as living on a vacant piece of property belonging to a higher status member of the family for the sole purpose of protecting it from squatters. Those of higher status may be asked to influence someone otherwise untouchable by the immediate family. These latter may be referred to again and again if they have achieved some honor, as election to the Senate or other political office. The associating members of the extended family constantly become involved in reciprocal relations that produce indebtedness to each other which by repayment and new indebtedness establish ties and loyalties that endure through many generations.

Affinal ties, established through marriage, are not by definition as strong as blood ties, but they may become so. For this to happen, there usually needs to be some consanguinal links in the past history of the families united by marriage. Marriage may bring peace to two previously hostile families.

## Ritual extensions of the family

Ritual extensions of the family bring non-blood related and non-affinal related people into a given family and make them the same as family. Such ritual extensions involve coparents of a child assigned at birth, at puberty (confirmation) and at marriage.

The ritual relationship is termed *compadrazgo* or "coparenthood". Coparents address each other as *comadre* or *compadre* depending upon the female sex or the male sex. The coparents or godparents become *padrinos de boda* at marriage or *padrinos de bautizo* at baptism.

Coparents at the wedding stand up for the bride and groom much as do the best man and the maid of honor at a North American one. They are frequently a married elder brother and his wife. They may be given enduring responsibilities, however, that the attendants at an American wedding do not have. For example, if the marriage turns sour, it is the responsibility of the coparents at marriage to try to resolve the conflict, much as the marriage counsellor works in North American society. They may also become responsible for the cost of the wedding depending on the agreement made prior to the wedding preparation.

Coparents at the baptism are selected from among the family's friends. For the second child, they may be selected from the wife's family. These coparents become responsible for the child in a number of distinct ways: 1) assist at the baptism, 2) buy the child's clothing for the baptismal ceremony and pay the officiating priest or minister's fee, 3) accompany the mother to *sacra misa* or the first mass forty days after the birth, 4) encourage the child in an adequate program of education, and 5) in the case of death, arrange for the wake, dress the body for burial and contribute to the funeral expense. In some areas it is also expected that the godparents present a yearly gift to the child at Christmas or on birthdays.

Godparents at the time of puberty or confirmation will assist in the ceremony of confirmation and may be called upon to punish the godchild in case of need. In some areas of Latin America this latter arrangement is not made. It is the least significant of the godparental arrangements.

Godparents address their godchildren in the familiar form of direct address, i.e. *tu* and are themselves addressed by *usted* or the respect form. Traditionally, the godchild kisses the hand of the godparent upon meeting. The child may also kneel before the parent or godparent. At such encounters of the godparent with the godchild the godparent may give the child a few pennies. There also exists a joking relationship between godparent and godchild which permits them to share a personal intimacy without any sexual overtones. It is much the same friendliness and comraderie that exists in North American society between the grandparent and grandchild.

Coparents address each other with the familiar form of direct address, i.e. *tu* or *vos* in a relationship of reciprocal respect, recognizing a high, though equal status in relationship to the coparented child. Coparents avoid intimacy or undue familiarity. For example, there may not be any discussion of sexual matters or there may be a covert expectation that coparents will not drink together. They may do favors for each other or borrow from each other, thus strengthening the ties between them but not to a degree that will lead to sexual opportunity.

The bond of coparenthood is more sacred than any personal tie outside the immediate family. This bond serves to provide security for the children much as insurance policies and investments made and willed to surviving children of the deceased do in North American society. The child has the confidence that he will have his needs met whatever happens to his parents.

In order to strengthen such security, parents who are poorer seek godparents for their children among the richer. Rural peoples look to the cities for the right godparents for their children, assuming that they can give greater aid in time of need. The more coparents a person has, the more people he has upon whom he can count for favors. This serves especially in the political realm, in providing a given candidate a pool of voters on whom he can rely with confidence. Naturally repayment is expected but there is no question but that this will and must be made.

The godparent thus relates to a given family in a highly privileged way. He can look to that family for support, and is even called upon for his potential influence over others, something a Latin loves to do. Further, he need fear no sexual involvement. Social control of the incest taboo operates in the relationship. As in North American society, siblings cannot marry each other; nor do parents and children; nor do godparents and godchildren. In a society of conquest and personal honor, this is a most significant factor in social relations. Finally, coparents are intimate in an honorary way within the family while being free of the trammels which bring dissension among kin.

Thus, there exists in Latin America a dual network of social relations that interlock and interpenetrate. This dual network extends any given Latin's contacts, influence and power into a variety of spheres, giving him an adequate foundation for social involvement with many contributions to his identity and security. His extended family and his coparent ritual extensions of family provide not only his primary socialization but also the matrix in which his personal life can be enriched.

## Case study re birth control

The average North American has come to appreciate and value the practice of birth control in his own culture. He frequently generalizes from his own experience and suggests or even demands that people of other cultures need it or must have it. Birth control practices in Spanish background societies are quite devastating when carried out irrespective of the sociocultural consequences. Birth control implies limiting people, and limiting them in relation to family. This is quite satisfactory within a society that wishes to provide maximum educational and economic foundations for each member of the family. The fewer children within the family, the more each will benefit educationally and economically, other things being equal.

The concern of the Latin is not so much educational and economic as person and personal identity. Person means other persons and personal identity is fulfilled within the social group which in his case is the family with its various extensions. Limiting the number of people thus implies limiting the people with whom a Latin can relate in terms of the deepest factors of identity. He stands to lose in areas of prestige if he has only one or two children. Each additional child he bears means additional opportunity for adding higher status persons to the family, as well as getting those children into higher status business and professional opportunities or into higher status families through marriage. He stands to lose in his own concept of personal manliness for there will be a limit to his progeny, visible evidence for his being a man. There will be a limit to those whom he can influence through his male stated authority; and also whom the mother can influence in the home.

Birth control, therefore, to the Latin, is the same as placing limitations on the insurance and investment potential of the North American. It strikes at the heart of power and influence within the family and larger community. It strikes further at their sense of self worth and fulfillment.

In a Latin American newspaper, a brief item reflects the reaction toward birth control:

> A newspaper cartoon shows the arms of Uncle Sam stretching across the border, spraying "babykill" at a Mexican baby carried in a sling from the beak of a startled stork.
> The cartoon has no caption and needs none. It expresses the bitter reaction of Mexicans to an American official's suggestion that birth control is needed south of the border.

# Chapter 9

# The Church

### Buildings of the church

The church is the most impressive building in any Latin American community. The first edifice one is likely to take note of is the church since it is the largest structure and the most prominent. Even in large cities, the church is more prominent and more highly visible than it is in North American cities. One can enter a large city, such as Chicago, in the United States and not have a sense of church at all. It is almost impossible to enter any city, of whatever size, in Latin America and not have a sense of church.

The Spanish pattern was to build the church in the central location in relation to the houses as well as to the public buildings of the community. Therefore, one will find the church on the central square occupying one full side of the square. There will also be some public building on another side of the square. This will be either the city hall or the state or national palace if the city is the capital of the state or nation. A third side of the square will be commercial with one or more business enterprises facing the public square. The final side is likely to be an extension of the park developed in the square, other public buildings, or commercial enterprises. Even if a Protestant church is located in the central area, it will probably be a block from the square rather than right on it. This is primarily due to its late arrival in the Latin community where the choice properties are established in families and these families, the church, and the public sector of the community, are reluctant to yield such choice properties.

The square will be a delightful park with flowers, shrubs and fountains, laid out and maintained by public institutions. The church benefits tremendously by being in the central area of the city.

The practice of the Spanish, again, was to construct the church and the associated buildings of the church (fellowship hall, educational building, priests' quarters) with durable materials. Therefore, the buildings are made of rock, much of it quarried so as to give the impression of large rock. The wooden parts of the structures are heavy beams and the roof is of galvanized metal roofing or slate shingles.

The interiors of the churches are reminiscent of the old world cathedrals with high ceilings, vast open spaces and a minimum of seating arrangements, especially in rural and semirural areas. Focus of the entire structure is on the altar which is large and ornate and extends across the entire front of the sanctuary. Frequently the walls and ceilings above the altar will be ornately decorated to extend the visual impact of the altar. Gold and gold leaf is widely used in ornamentation.

Even though the church building is very prominent in the Latin community and catches one's attention immediately upon entering, it is not long before it becomes apparent that the church is multi-edifice. The "city-center" building is only one of a number of associated edifices of the church. The second most prominent is called *calvario* or "calvary". It is generally located on a rise or knoll in juxtaposition to the main edifice (if this is possible) so that a person standing on the steps of the church in town can look directly out to calvary. It generally takes only a few minutes to walk from the church to calvary's hill where there is a chapel of smaller proportions than the church, and frequently a cemetery where the members of the community are buried. There may be services in the chapel, but it is used primarily in funerals as a center for prayer. In larger towns and cities, the church-calvary complex were bypassed and now calvary, which was primarily a peripheral structure in relation to the town, has become integral and is mistaken for another church by the uninitiated.

The shrine and its attendant chapel is a third major edifice of the church in Latin America. This can be located anywhere there was evidence of a miracle. At the site of the miracle, or as close to it as the terrain permitted, a chapel would be built and perhaps a priest's quarters.

When the Spanish priests entered a community in the northern highlands of Guatemala, the Indians were practicing their particular religions and making use of small figurines made of jade. A number of these found their way into the church and became a part of the worship experience. A new priest entered this particular community after many decades of established religious syncretistic practices and sought to purify the practices of the Indian peoples. He ordered the jade figurines destroyed and sent a small group of Indian men to the mountains to crush and demolish them. The men were reluctant to destroy that which had come to them at the hands of their fathers and so simply threw them into a bushy area. A miracle occurred which is described no further in the folklore of the area. Upon their return to the town they revealed what had happened to the priest and he immediately went out and established a rude chapel. This was later moved to a more accessible location and a large permanent structure was built. One of the large wings of the chapel contains wall plaques telling in detail the various miracles of healing and strengthening that have attended pilgrimages to the shrine. The shrine is named very appropriately *chi ixim* or "to the corn" since the only impression that the local people had of the miracle involved light and corn, the primary staple of the area.

Besides these more established structures, there will be shrines established at crossroads, along the side of the road where something special has happened, or at some unique part of the terrain as at a waterfall or in a cave or grotto. Besides the shrines, the houses of the *mayordomos* or lay leaders of the church community will have an altar decorated from time to time in conjunction with a religious festival.

The church bell dominates the community; it can be heard anywhere in the area.

**The priest**

The priest is biological man but sociological priest. As biological man, he has all the needs felt by anyone else in the community. He must eat, and so will have a cook who will prepare his food for him. He must sleep and so will have quarters connected to the church. He has sexual urges and so may establish sexual liaisons with certain women, while fulfilling his obligations of celibacy.

As sociological priest, however, he is set apart to the service of the church. He is the faithful representative of Christ on earth and the perception of such faithfulness is maintained corporately. Faithfulness is defined not so much in terms of what one does not do as is the North American practice, but rather in terms of fulfilling that which is by definition, the work of the priest. He is the divinely appointed authority of Christ on earth so his word is law. It is not to be contradicted in any way and serious sanctions are placed upon any who question such authority and the priest's right to it. The priest is further above manliness, so he has no particular internal drive to conquer woman, though these same drives are turned toward Mary and a deepening sense of loyalty to her. He is a-status. The priest is above the status system operating in Latin society in the sense that wherever he is placed in his ministry, he will always be the highest status person in that church-related community. Whenever a Protestant pastor is placed in a new parish, there is the period of adjustment that always takes place with each member of the religious community evaluating his own status in relation to the pastor. If certain members of the church decide that the pastor is below them in status, they are very likely to lose interest in the church program and may even withdraw and form a new church that will "meet their needs". This can never happen in the Catholic community. The priest is received immediately as above anyone else in status and he can immediately get on with the tasks of his ministry. To the degree that the civil government is tied to the church, the priest will be of higher status than the government officials. In nations that are extremely Catholic in their orientation, the highest status priest in the hierarchy will be above the president in status and can thus dominate him.

Were the priest to marry or enter a business enterprise, he would immediately be tied to the status system operating in the larger society. His status level would then be determined on the basis of the status level of his family of origin, that of his new bride's family, or of the level of status of his business. This determination of status rank could seriously affect his ministering to people who might then see themselves as higher status than the priest. It could completely destroy his ministry and that for which he stood.

## The member

To be Latin is to be Catholic. As soon as a child is born it is enrolled in the church. To become something other than Catholic is to take definitive action to renounce Catholicism and embrace a new religion. Only those who take such definitive action are ever considered as other than Catholic.

The member of the church is an isolate. That which he is and does is always in relation to the church, the priest, and the altar—all are one and the same by symbolic representation. This is not to say that the member is treated as an individual, with individual rights as would be the case in North America. Rather, the member relates unidirectionally for faith, support, salvation or anything else that the church has for him. He does not relate in the group. He is not a cipher without a sense of person. Rather, he is seen as a person with personal responsibilities directed in only one way, toward the church and all it stands for. That which is for the good of the church is for the good of the person and that which is for the good of the person is for the good of the church.

Reciprocity is therefore in terms of an imbalance rather than in terms of role equality. The priest is authority personified and the member is non-authority. Instruction moves from the priest to the parishioner.

A LOOK AT LATIN AMERICAN LIFESTYLES

Grace is meted out from source to receiver. The member is never anything other than receiver.

Participation within the context of the church is therefore designed by response rather than initiation. During the mass, correct response to the cues insures an adequate experience. At the times of the life crises, birth, puberty, marriage and death, proper response to the activities required insures peace and privilege. He who initiates is repressed and controlled. Excommunication from the church, which in its impact means reduction to nothing or to "vegetable" insofar as society is concerned, is the ultimate sanction. Message is heard and obeyed, not formed. It is directed by way of monologue so that the official representative can initiate it and all others can receive. The Bible is seen in this relationship also as that which serves the initiator and not the receiver. It is only when the initiator gives permission that the receiver may utilize the Bible. Any use of the Bible as initiator, apart from the stated authority, is a threat to the authority and therefore to the entire system.

Group involvement is not in terms of the members relating to members, rather of group relating as isolate in the same non-reciprocating, unidirectional way as the individual does. In the Protestant church it is impossible for a person or group not to interact with another person or with another group within the confines of the buildings and the scope of the organization. People pray together in groups, they sing and worship in such a way that they are aware of those about them, in a way that helps them make contact with those about them. By definition, the group is made up of certain people, families, or interest blocs within the whole. Even North American Catholics are influenced by this and one finds their participation in the church quite distinct from that of the Catholic in Latin America. In fact, at times, a North American Catholic would find himself totally disoriented within a Latin American Catholic setting.

Such a pattern of relationships is to be expected within a status-ranked society. With everyone on a different level of status, an institution could not operate unless its members could interact or not interact with others when they chose. The Protestant interpenetration of relationships at every level of the society is not only a threat, therefore, to the church and its practices, but to the entire society as well. When you become a member of a Protestant church, or even visit, you must relate to others within the setting, if it means only a greeting and handshake at the door. Social egalitarianism takes hold at that moment and is reinforced constantly through the experience with the church.

**The income of the church**

The income of the church is always pegged to status and one's expected ability to pay. A contribution must therefore be in keeping with the known status-wealth level of the person making the contribution. Anything less is seen as niggardly and is an immediate alarm sounded in relation to potential loss of status within the community. Anything more than one's expected level of contribution is evidence of social climbing. The two become disruptive within Latin society. The former lowers the status of associates; and the latter becomes a threat to those of higher status since such a challenge may result in their loss of status.

All services of the church, made available to its members, are ranked in keeping with the status-wealth level of the member. A baptism, involving the same activities and ritual will carry a higher fee to the higher status and a lower fee to a lower status member. Generally, the person paying more receives more in the way of ritual and personal satisfaction but this is a side benefit, rather than an inherent part of the system. The Protestant, not paying any particular attention to status, assures its adherents that all the grace of the church is free and everyone receives back from the church the same as everyone else. Privilege is in terms of maturity rather than social stratification. This leaves the characteristic Latin quite uncomfortable in the Protestant program since he is unsure of himself and of his God. The Protestant expects little financial remuneration and receives little. The Catholic expects that each will pay according to his ability and never seems to be lacking in funds.

## The ritual

The ritual of the church is administered weekly as the *misa* or mass, and at times of festival. The weekly mass is offered numerous times during the weekend and the only stipulation to the adherents of the church is that they participate at least once a week. Associated with the mass may be confession or other related activities but each is to get one ready for the mass and are therefore satellite activities.

Rituals during the life crises festivals of birth, puberty, marriage and death usually involve the mass as well, but it is only part of a larger complex of activity and ritual. The rite of baptism is usually performed about five to eleven days following birth. The rites of puberty are called confirmation and occur sometime during the twelfth or thirteenth year of the child. The rituals of marriage take place following the civil wedding and involve a reception either before or after the church ceremony. The death rituals involve a wake during the first night following the death, a funeral procession and burial rites usually led by the priest, and a wake held one year from the death date.

Ritual of the church is scaled according to status and to distance. Those of higher status are able to have more opportunities for the services of

# A LOOK AT LATIN AMERICAN LIFESTYLES

the church and the rituals are generally more elaborate. Those geographically nearer the church with resident priest are available for more of the services of the church than those farther away. Geographically removed persons, who do not get to the church building itself, may receive the ministrations of the church only yearly or a few times during their lifetime.

In one area of the central highlands of Guatemala, the people had to guarantee the priest a chicken dinner to get him into their area which was three hours by trail from the church. Frequently, when people would know that I was to go out on the trails, even though I was a professional anthropologist and linguist, they would tease me by asking, "Have you arranged for your chicken dinner"?

Religious rituals also attend the larger community and its activities. They are not specifically related to the church building but do have integral ties with the Catholic religion. These include the festival and the pilgrimage. The festival calendar is oriented to sacred days. There are four categories of festival occasions in the larger Latin community and five in any community including Indian people. Church holidays are tied to the life and times of Jesus Christ. These are festivals such as Good Friday, Christmas, Corpus Cristi, etc. There are also the saint's days of the corporate bodies called *cofradias* or lay brotherhoods. In the average community there will likely be one brotherhood with its assigned saint's day for each calendar month. Some communities will have as few as eight such festivals a year and others will have as many as two per month. It is on the saint's day that the religious brotherhood honors its own patron saint and carries out the primary activities of the brotherhood. Each individual has his own saint and it is on his birthday that he honors this particular saint. He is assigned to the saint by being born on the day traditionally assigned that saint. There are also festivals joining church and state such as the various national holidays during which there are always religious activities in the form of processions and special masses. Perhaps one of the most important of these is the town festival honoring the date of origin of the town. The brotherhood assigned to this date generally becomes the most important of the brotherhoods of that particular community. Indian holidays are added in Indian areas.

The pilgrimage can be one of two types. In one the person goes to the place of residence of the saint and in the other the saint is carried to the person. Each Latin nation has one special saint that is either the patron saint or has achieved some special place in the life of the larger community. For example, the Black Christ of Esquipulas, though not the patron saint of Guatemala, is perhaps the most significant to the average Guatemalan. There is a shrine in the eastern city of Esquipulas where the Black Christ resides, which people pledge themselves to visit at least once during their lifetime. There will be yearly excursions to Esquipulas from all parts of the country as people arrange for chartered busses and go en masse. There might also be the lone pilgrimage as the result of a crisis in the life, such as the death of a loved one, or on the eve of a special occasion.

From time to time, the Black Christ of Esquipulas is carried throughout the country. Such a pilgrimage for the image representing the saint is of special significance to the people along the route. They will throw money into the coffer or large box on which the saint is placed, and men will pay for the special privilege of carrying the saint one or more blocks. Saints with lesser influence will be carried through their own region and local saints will be carried through town during the particular processions when this is appropriate.

## The woman and the church

The woman is a very important person in the Latin American religious life. She is likely to be the most active and loyal adherent of the church. It is not uncommon for the woman to never miss the regular services of the church even as it is not uncommon for the man to miss most of them. The primary role of instruction of her children in the Catholic faith falls to the woman. Their understanding of the church doctrine and their attendance at training programs and at mass are her responsibility and under her supervision. The contentment of the priest within a given parish is correlated with the support and encouragement he receives from the women of the parish. Finally, the priest is attended to by women. His cook is likely to be any local woman who can cook to suit his tastes. However, the woman that attends to his quarters and to special needs, such as birthday celebrations, is one of the high status married women of the community. She is honored to be selected for such a duty and her behavior, whatever might attend her association with the priest, is unquestioned. If she has a child by the priest, that child will be received unquestioningly within the home. The community will corporately ignore the child's special origin. This is particularly true if the priest is well liked.

Julian Pitt-Rivers has quite succinctly stated the place and power of the church in Latin life: "Though the pueblo tends to show hostility to the temporal order of the church, the powers of religion play an all-important part in its institutions, and indeed its solidarity is expressed in its relation to the patron saint." (Pitt-Rivers 1961.)

A LOOK AT LATIN AMERICAN LIFESTYLES

## For further reading

Cutler, Donald R., ed. *The Religious Situation:* 1969, Beacon Press, Boston, 1969.

Greene, Graham, *The Power and the Glory,* The Viking Press, N.Y., 1958.

Landsberger, Henry, *The Church and Social Change in Latin America,* University of Notre Dame Press, London, 1970.

Maryknoll Documentation Series, *Between Honesty and Hope,* Maryknoll Publications, Maryknoll, N.Y., 1969.

Mecham, J. Lloyd, *Church and State in Latin America,* Chapel Hill, The University of North Carolina Press, 1966.

Pitt-Rivers, Julian, *The People of the Sierra,* University of Chicago Press, Chicago, 1961.

Ryan, Edwin, *The Church in the South American Republics,* Bruce Publishing Company, N.Y., 1932.

# Chapter 10

# The Military

Even as the church is more highly visible in Latin America than it is in North America, the military is also. There is hardly a parade held in any large center that does not include a military detachment. Military men are in every public building for some reason or other. One encounters service personnel on the highways both in travel and at traffic control checkpoints.

## Structural types of armed forces in Latin America

There are four structural types of armed forces in Latin America: the regular army, paramilitary units, the private army, and the people's armies. There are occasions when they are maintained completely separate, which is the normal course of affairs. There are other occasions when any or all are merged. When Castillo Armas sought to enter Guatemala during the late fifties, he developed a people's army which took in, during a march on Guatemala City, units of the regular army under the leadership of regular army personnel, and some paramilitary forces collected along the route. There have been other times when a private army became the main force within the regular army with the leader's accession to the presidency of the nation.

The regular army is dominant, even if it is not always the most powerful. The armed forces of the regular army are under the domination of the government and consist of the army, the navy and the air force. The army is the dominant force in the regular armed forces and is usually able to maintain its authority in the military and reinforce its power in any situation. The navy is characteristically weak, but since Latin American societies tend to be traditional societies and relate institutions to their traditional roles and place within the larger society, the navy has been able to maintain its high status yielding only to the land forces. The air force, though potentially powerful, is maintained as a service organization within the military and as such finds its overall power limited. Very few altercations between the army and the air force find the air force winning out. One reason for this is that the core of the air force is made up of pilots who are kept busy flying military planes, civilian cargo and civilian or government sponsored passenger planes. Further, their bases are distributed throughout the nation, and there is seldom one central base of power within the country where a power play can be made. Finally, their equipment, since it is quite expensive, is kept to a minimum due to the financial problems characteristic of Latin nations. The equipment is usually older and not always in top repair.

The paramilitary forces are regional armies that may be civic action groups. They are under control of the government as are the regular armed forces and may be commissioned as regular army at any moment of national crisis. One of the best known expressions of paramilitary force is the local police.

Anyone in Latin America can have a private army as long as he can afford to sustain it. The more protection the regular army or paramilitary units can effect under government control, the less need there is of a private army. Whenever such protection is lacking, private armies spring up all the way from the informal type of arming the farmhands to specially outfitted and uniformed bodyguard teams or armies. Wealthy men or political leaders in remote areas, such as governors of remote states, provinces, or departments, will develop a private army which will dominate the entire area since national protective forces are not readily available. The Brazilian coup of 1964 was effected by the use of a private army. Adhemar de Barro commanded some 40,000 troups during the uprising which deposed the Goulart regime.

The people's armies are generally guerrilla insurgents. Their leaders are drawn from the urban sectors and are generally idealists and high achievers. They are not usually military men. Castillo Armas led a successful revolutionary force into Guatemala and forced a change in government there even as Fidel Castro did a few years later in Cuba. The followers of these dynamic and often charismatic leaders are recruited from the rural peasantry. They serve in these armies in order to right some wrong, or to redress an evil they perceive to exist within society.

## Functions of the military

The military in Latin America has four primary functions: the defense of national territory, the support of the constitution, the maintenance of internal order and social effort. In fulfilling each and all of these functions, the military has become one of the two conservative forces in Latin American society standing alongside the church in maintaining a national identity.

In Latin America, international territorial struggle is at a minimum. Nevertheless, the military is ready, though not always adequately prepared, to defend the national territory. Even though actual struggle is at a minimum, each nation has some border dispute with an adjoining nation. Mexico had it with the United States. Guatemala has a continuing dispute with Belice or British Honduras. Peru and Ecuador have one of the border disputes that flares up more than the average. The feeling in Belice runs so high that even during a typhoon that wiped out part of the nation, they still refused aid offered by Guatemala since it would have been carried in by military forces. They would rather do without the aid than run the risk of takeover by the Guatemalan military entering under the guise of an errand of mercy. In fact, anyone naming Belice by its other name, British Honduras, in public in Guatemala can very quickly be turned upon by the Guatemalans and could ultimately be considered persona non grata in Guatemala.

The military is pledged to the support of the constitution. This refers not to the present, stated form of the constitution, but rather to the original contract on which the nation as a nation is based. Whenever the military feels that the civilian government is operating in any way contrary to that original contract, it will move in and take over the government and in time restore the government to civilian rule. During that period, however, the present written form of the constitution will be withdrawn or revoked and a new form presented to the nation. Then when it chooses to or when it is no longer powerful enough to maintain its rule it will transfer power back to the people and their duly selected leaders. One of the primary reasons for political instability in Latin America is that the military has enough power to prevent governments from ruling that are unfavorable to it (and to the constitution by implication) but not enough power to rule for any length of time. In Latin America twenty to fifty years is not considered an especially long period of time in terms of national sovereignty.

The armed forces feel they have this right to interfere in the course of government since they are the incarnation of the nation and guardians of national virtues and traditions. This has developed a consistent belief in Latin America that the use of the military is justifiable for the preservation of patriotism if not politics. What frequently happens, however, is that the military winds up being the preserve of national tradition and class privilege.

The military is also empowered to maintain internal order. In each nation, it is the unique guarantor of sovereignty, however much it might be indebted to foreign support to accomplish this purpose. It is in the maintenance of internal order that the regular army and the paramilitary forces are frequently united. Numerous outsiders have been slain ignoring the orders of local policemen during periods of military rule and marshall law. They have overlooked the fact that the local police have been taken into the army for this national crisis and function as full military with its rights and privileges. They can therefore shoot to kill whenever their orders are ignored.

The military may in a given nation carry out more of a social role than a military one. Wherever Latins and Indians are within the same sociogeographic zone the military tend to bring the two together in social intercourse. They carry out programs of education, or technical training and the like. Within their force itself there is a break with traditional class and caste barriers though this is seldom translated into private life. There is advance for the lowly by the merit system that does work to a degree. Finally there is progress in transportation and communication networks that serve the entire nation.

These functions are carried out through programs supporting geographical institutions, sponsoring surveys and mapping, and through linguistic studies. The military open frontier areas for colonization and aid in making these programs successful. They establish and maintain transportation systems by air or land and set up communication centers in all parts of the nation, both urban and rural. They carry out programs of reforestation, of public health, disaster relief, and literacy in conjunction with other educational programs.

## Political role of the military

The military has become a professional force under civilian rule in some Latin countries such as Mexico, Uruguay and Costa Rica, where it operates much as it does in the United States and Canada. In other nations, it has become a political force involving a number of types: the caudillistic form, the trustee form, the orienter form, the consensual form and the veto form.

In the caudillistic form of a political military, the national leader is invariably an officer in the armed forces such as Juan Perón was in Argentina. In the trustee form the power resides in the military but party politics are allowed to exist in the civilian style. In the orienter form, deviant forms of politics are prevented from seizing power but traditionalist or constitutionalist norms are not interfered with. In the consensual form, civilian government exists with the tacit consent of, but with minimum interference from, the military. In the veto forms of political involvement, the military acts as a faction in and for itself but otherwise is without political power. Over a period of time, each nation may have all in its life span and one expression today may yield to another expression tomorrow.

In Latin America, there is little evidence to support the view of the military as a democratic force. For one thing, there is a persistence of traditional patterns of culture inherited from the agrarian feudal society. When the military is defending the constitution, it is defending this traditional pattern of behavior. It thus uses constitutionalism for conservative ends. Its power becomes a legal limit to personal sovereignty rather than a guarantee for maximum personal liberty. This results quite naturally in a continuation of class interests. Finally, the ecological factor or reality of Latin nationhood contributes to political instability and power plays undermining the democratic process. The coasts are well settled and heavily developed whereas the rural and interior regions are sparsely settled. This is due to the mountainous or jungle nature of the terrain throughout most of Latin America. Military concentrations are close to the vital centers thus encouraging coups that disrupt the natural electoral process.

In Latin America, the land forces dominate on the military scene. The social role they fulfill is equally important, if not more so in ultimately benefiting the nation. The military is a strong enough political force to serve the nation and its constitution, but not strong enough to maintain control for a long period of time. Finally, along with the church, the military becomes the most conservative force in Latin life seeking to maintain the original social contract on which its national life is based.

## For further reading

Horowitz, Irving Louis, "The Military Elites" in Lipset and Solari, *Elites in Latin America,* Oxford University Press, N.Y., 1967.

Johnson, John J., "The Soldier as Citizen and Bureaucrat" in Robert D. Tomasek, *Latin American Politics,* Doubleday and Co., N.Y., 1966.

Lieuwen, Edwin, "The Changing Role of the Armed Forces: An Analysis" in Tomasek, *Latin American Politics,* 1966.

McAlister, Lyle N., "The Military" in John J. Johnson, *Continuity and Change in Latin America,* Stanford University Press, Stanford, 1964.

# Chapter 11

# Government

The primary key to government in Latin America lies in the interlocking and interpenetrating extended families. Whereas, in North America, North Americans relate to government as individual isolates, i.e. voting, paying taxes, etc., the Latin relates to government as family.

Two processes are constantly at work to mold and limit government: the consultation of heads of extended families, and the maintenance of the extended family by the women. These are two powerful forces, operating mostly covertly, that determine just what a given form of government will do. The extended family cannot dictate, it cannot form an overt power block, nor can it do many of the surface things that would be involved in decision making such as form a law or try a criminal. These are not the strengths of the extended family. The primary strength of families, rather, is the resistance to policy, action, deed, and process. The government is unable to carry out its work effectively unless the extended families, or at least a majroity of these, are on the side of government. Such resistance to policy and action growing from policy not only leaves programming in jeopardy but also leaves the government with the aura of weakness, which in a Latin setting is very bad indeed.

Extended families are focused on their leader who is the eldest male that retains physical strength and mental acumen. This is likely the father or grandfather leading a family of married sons and daughters, each with their own nuclear families. If the eldest male has not survived or is physically unable to function, the family may look to the man's wife for such leadership. She does not have all the extended political and governmental opportunities that the man might have but the effect is still the same—she can express resistance to policy and action that is ultimately felt in the seats of government.

The process of election of political leaders sets up this network of extended families within the strata-rank system of stratification. No political aspirant has any hope of success until he recruits support. The way he does this is to enter an extended family and by this association make or promise some provision for some need or needs of the family. He enters another in the same way, not forcing the two to interrelate and merge as one, but to maintain its own separate identity and relate only if there are ties of marriage or ritual relations. He develops his relationships with the leaders of the extended families through reciprocal aid and favors until he has their loyalty. Once he has the loyalty of a given leader, he can be assured of the loyalty of most of the extended families related to that leader by blood, affinal or ritual ties and any associated families which are lower in status. This mini-network is put together with others (never forcing the interrelation but deriving the loyalty) until the political aspirant has sufficient power to win an election. The moment he wins, he is indebted to the network of extended families that made his election to office possible and now continues the reciprocal favor extending practice and pays close attention to their wishes so that the ties of loyalty are not broken. These loyalty ties extend through many generations and are thus important to maintain. Any politician contesting the results of an election is not questioning the actual counting of the ballots. Rather, he examines the list of expected voters committed and then questions whether they actually did or did not vote for him. If it is clear that he should have had the number of votes to win, he will insist on the laborious process of a revote. The entire process may take until the next election and some politicians have remained in office during an entire term when there has been good reason to question a given vote.

## Weak central government

The overall effect of government tied to interlocking extended families is to produce a weak central government. The central government can only move as fast as the vast network of extended families permits. The alternate effect is to reinforce local governments serving much closer to the actual extended families involved. This has the effect of developing local strongmen who dominate their sociogeographical zones as virtual dictators and who can maintain this strength through the hiring of private armies. The strongman who becomes powerful enough may in time become president of the nation, but he at least can impose his will on his area for many decades without interference from the national government.

There are two clear evidences in the behavior patterns of Latin Americans to confirm such a practice. The first of these is in the matter of police protection and the other in the pattern of architecture termed "Spanish". Because of a strong central government in North America, there is an umbrella of protection for the citizen that extends throughout the nation, with certain pockets unprotected such as a given park in a large city or certain neighborhoods in a deteriorating urban setting. Such is not true in Latin America. Upper status homes are bound to be robbed at some time during the lifetime of the family unless there is an armed guard or some protection given. In other words, the upper status person can expect to be robbed in Latin America whereas he can expect not to be robbed in North America. It is by chance that the Latin American escapes whereas it is by chance that the North American suffers.

Since the Latin American national government cannot guarantee the security of the citizenry, the citizen himself must take this responsibility. There are more house guards, neighborhood guards, private goon or bodyguard forces, and private armies in Latin America than could ever be dreamed of in North America. It simply signifies the inability of the national government to effectively protect its citizenry.

Spanish architecture which calls for the edifice to be built around the edge of the property rather than in the center of the property as is the North American style is further evidence of a lack of a strong central government. The protection this affords the family or the enterprise is equivalent to that provided by the walled city. The outsider has a difficult time entering the confines of the family dwelling finding only the front door or the back wall as means of access. The front door faces the street and the back wall is edged with spikes of glass to make entry more difficult. No windows remain unbarred and the family dwelling, though attractively maintained through the use of patio flowers and color, is actually a fortress in miniature.

## The clerk

The central government is strengthened internally, in spite of its weakness externally, by its clerks. Latin American government is run by clerks and these frequently are women.

These clerks are not so much typists and file clerks as administrative clerk-secretaries. They carry a great deal of responsibility for the paper work of the governmental process. They also carry a great deal of the weight of government in personal contact in the office. They are not so much administrative secretaries, in the North American sense, since they do not especially relate to a staff below them. But they serve more as a go-between for the head or politician and the public.

There are at least three processes at work that produce this phenomenon. The first of these is the need of the Latin for an intermediary. The intermediary comes to have more power than the boss, simply because the intermediary can do what he or she wishes with the message carried—turn it to the favor of the public or turn it against the public. In other words, the decision may pretty much be made before the elected official or the boss is approached. The second process involves the electoral process and the ease by which a public official is removed from office. The elected official is there for his term of office. The clerk is there for life or as long as he or she can function in that position. Thus the clerk knows what is going on and can manipulate the elected official according to his pleasure. Thirdly, the woman has a subtle but powerful control over the male. Since the largest number of the elected officials are male, and the clerks are primarily female, the effect is not only to reinforce the power of the intermediary but also to insure the woman's presence in the office for as long a time as possible.

## The formal nature of government

The business of government in Latin America is carried out more formally than in North America. Matters of dress, protocol, request, etc., require attention to formalities not demanded or expected in North America.

The expectations in dress can be summarized in the statement, "you dress up to the level of the very highest status possible for you". Thus, when a rural peasant goes to a government office of any kind he wears his Sunday best. This will consist of a black coat and light pants and his best shirt, though no tie. It is still his very best outfit and the black coat is a must. By the time he moves through the status levels, the expectation is a full black suit, a clean white shirt, a well knotted tie, and black shoes well shined. The darker the clothes, the more accepted he is in circles of government. This best dress is what he wears at all important occasions such as a high mass in his religious life, the funeral of a highly respected community leader in the community life or the important business engagement in his economic life. For the woman, her best dress is called for and this will usually also be dark and conservative.

In keeping with the status system of Latin America, the higher one's status, the greater the entree. The political figure is of quite high status in the community. Anyone who can maintain or achieve the perception of higher status than the official can be welcomed by the official at any time and is likely to receive all that he wishes. The moment one is perceived on a lower status level than the official, he loses this immediate entree. He must then work through the system to accomplish his purposes, either giving a gift to reflect loyalty to the official, calling in an intermediary loyal to him through blood or ritual ties who is higher in status than the official, or by making use of the clerk in the office as an intermediary. In the case of the latter, a good relationship must be maintained with the clerk and he or she must be kept apprised of the activities of the person or group making a request.

In a society in which members protect themselves from error or the appearance of error (see Chapter 14), paper work becomes vitally important. Thus red tape in the sense of thoroughgoing paper and file work becomes an integral part of government. It is not possible to receive a response to a request when the request is made. The request is processed at the speed the paper work is accomplished. Action is taken after all the papers are in hand and signed by the proper official. Very frequently, the choice must be made by the person involved in government contact, between standing in line or hiring an agent to represent his interests.

The North American is taken aback in Latin America because he personally must become more involved in eliciting decisions on matters, many of which he was uninvolved in his homeland; and because of the degree to which paperwork becomes visible in the process of eliciting this decision. It is just enough more to irritate him until he begins to work with the system. A comparable example is the additional call for the personal handshake in Latin America. It is not called for that much more, but enough so that the North American, at the early stages of contact with the Latin American often forgets to put out his hand until he sees the Latin persist in offering his. On returning to his own society, he finds himself extending his hand at times that elicits surprise or a startled response from the one he is greeting.

## The Latin as political

The Latin is political in the same way that the North American is socioeconomic. The early conversation of two North Americans during a normal period of life would likely focus on some recreational, athletic, social, educational or economic opportunity or interest. The early conversation of the Latin is likely to be political. Later on the North American might get around to political interests but the Latin tends to home in on these almost immediately. When invited to speak to a group on North American lifestyles, the North American is likely to talk most of the time on other than political concerns. The Latin, in the same situation, would likely dwell more on political concerns and less on others.

The two periods of his life when he is most political in his interests and in the expenditure of his energies are when he is in advanced education such as late high school or university and when he has achieved a certain age and power base from this advanced age and the prestige it has brought him. During his university life, politics plays a very important role in his education. Formal education will usually yield to political interests whether it is for the sake of a demonstration, or when the professors wish to pursue political interests. School will close down or studies will come second to the primary political concerns.

Government is carried out under the limitations of the interpenetrating extended families leaving central government weak in relation to stronger local government. Clerks play a very important part in government which makes for certain formalities.

## For further reading

Adams, Richard N., *Crucifixion by Power,* University of Texas Press, Austin, 1970.
Busey, James L., *Latin America (Political Institutions and Processes),* Random House, N.Y., 1964.
Denton, Charles F., *Patterns of Costa Rican Politics,* Allyn and Bacon, Inc., Boston, 1971.
Snow, Peter, *Political Forces in Argentina,* Allyn and Bacon, Inc., Boston, 1971.
Tomasek, Robert D., *Latin American Politics,* Doubleday and Co., N.Y., 1966.
von Lazar, Arpad, *Latin American Politics: a Primer,* Allyn and Bacon, Inc., Boston, 1971.
Williams, Mary W., *The People and Politics of Latin America,* Ginn and Co., Boston, 1930.

# Chapter 12

# The Woman

Eugene Nida (1957) distinguishes Latin America as a woman oriented society from a society that is sex oriented. By now, the reader has a new appreciation of the place of the woman in Latin society. The woman is in focus in every aspect of the society. Hers is a covert, low key focus around which the entire society revolves.

This is not to say that the Latin woman is not a sex object. Her sexual attraction is great and becomes most prominent in her relationship to the male in machismo. Further, it is caught up in concepts of beauty as in selection of plumpness over slenderness and darkness over lightness. Finally it is quite an obvious factor in flirtation, something that is carried out much more overtly in Latin America than in North America. Male eyes follow the female figure much more obviously in Latin America than in North America. The joke about the Latin male bumping into the pole while ogling a female is a joke based on fact.

Far more significant to the total operation of the society, however, is the woman's place in the warp and woof of Latin life, and the deeply meaningful nature of woman as an authority figure. This is not the kind of thing that shows, that is flaunted, or that is even admitted in certain sectors of the society. It is more like an artesian well that lies mostly below the surface and extends deeply into the ground but when it does surface, it is with a force that shows great vitality and does not permit stagnation.

It takes the woman to reveal the manliness of the male in Latin society. Without the woman, there would be no one to conquer. Without the progeny of the wife and mistress, there would not be that substantive evidence of virility. Again, this is not something that is flaunted, since the result of flaunting the manliness and its evidences destroys its effect—a highly significant social control to maintain the society in balance. However, take note of the fantastic bargaining position in which this places the woman. If she yields to the male, he is fulfilled as a man. If she refuses, he remains unfulfilled, a nothing in relation to the entire society. It pays the man to do everything necessary to gain the favor of the woman. A bargain is therefore likely to be struck at the point of marriage, at the time of intercourse, and at the moment of decision in every matter needing the involvement of the woman. The man is unable to control the full content and force of the bargain, but the woman is not under the same limitation. The woman, it is true, needs a male child for her own fulfillment, and there are social pressures for her to marry early, but she still enjoys a slight advantage over the man.

The woman's presence adds a verve to life that is not realizable in any other way. Her presence on the street makes her the object of intense, but not sensually serious flirtation. To the outsider it appears sensuous in comparison to his own social system, but to the Latin it is more sport—an end in itself, rather than means to an end. There are numerous other routes to achieve conquest and though flirtation may be utilized in achieving those ends, it is a secondary route. This shows when a young girl, raised in a Latin community, returns to her North American homeland and flirts in keeping with her Latin acculturation. The reaction of the North American male is that she is really loose and eager, whereas in reality she is simply more aggressive in flirtation, but not necessarily in sexual intent. The woman's presence in the office or in the home has this same effect. To a degree not realized in North America, the house without a woman is not a home at all. In fact, it is impossible for the characteristic Latin to conceive of a house without a woman. To have a woman or a man living alone, or two men living by themselves is something incomprehensible to the Latin. It must certainly indicate motivation based on sensual desire, rather than on some pure, responsible motivation.

The woman has the real authority even though the man has the stated authority. After the man has stated his wishes and left the house, the woman does as she intended originally. The children see the woman and her actions in relation to the words of their father and discover that the mother is really more to be reckoned with. This process takes many years, but since the woman is supervising her children to the age of puberty, about twelve or thirteen, and the girls long after that, the reinforcement of act on act makes it an incontrovertible fact.

The paired concept of manliness-female honor indicates the woman as the source of honor and reputation in the home. This is extended into every aspect of Latin life, for she takes this reputation wherever she goes.

## A LOOK AT LATIN AMERICAN LIFESTYLES

In the church, since she is the main participant, this becomes a deeply meaningful thing as a type of Mary, the woman of highest honor and reputation. In the nation, this becomes a concept of ultimate honor of nationhood in a society conceiving of nationhood as female rather than male as we do in the United States. By her actions, the woman maintains her reputation or loses it. She is free to do whatever she pleases just so she does not reveal the wrong (by Latin definition) things. This reputation becomes a primary concern for the men of the community and nation for if the woman as mother, sister or wife loses her reputation, the value to the male, of his manliness, is of little value. If the nation, as female, loses her reputation, of what value is life at all? If the person of Mary, as the primary intermediary between God and man, loses her reputation, of what importance are the deeper meanings of life? Only despair is left.

Thus, the woman becomes the primary source for stability in the Latin experience. In the family, she is always there, making those decisions that the members of the family need for their everyday—and most immediately significant—sensory experiences. Within the extended family, as the one who is responsible for maintaining the good relationships within the family, her influence extends far beyond the family. Being primarily responsible for the continuing contentment of the priest, she exercises a vital stabilizing role in this institution that is so totally identified with Latin life. With the nation seen as female, especially the constitution, the military is set for the defense of the constitution, of the nation and thus of woman. Each of these aspects of Latin society is rooted in the stabilizing influence of the woman who, in a covert but powerful way, can determine the destiny of man and of nation.

Woman, as clerk, runs the machinery of government. She is wanted in terms of her presence. She knows all that is going on since the operations of government pass through her hands. She serves as the intermediary in the finely balanced system of favor granting and reciprocal relations. She is likely to be there for a longer period of time than is the boss or the official. Her integral and enduring place in government is not to be taken lightly, but must be dealt with by those within the society as well as by those without.

She becomes involved with government less directly, but just as significantly when, upon the death of a head of an extended family, she becomes the leader. Though unable to have direct and immediate input in government, her influence is felt in her direction of resistance to policy and action. Very frequently also, she controls not only the money of the family but influences the money expenditure in a larger network of family and extended family.

Perhaps, more than any other influence exerted on Latin life by the woman is her role as intermediary. She serves as intermediary between father and child, between nuclear head of family and head of extended family, between boss and underling, between child and future family, between asker of favor and grantor of favor. As intermediary, she becomes a type of ultimate intermediary, namely Mary in her relationship as intermediary between God and man. The Latin knows deep in his very being that the very best intermediary is the woman, and that if he can sway the woman, all favors will come to him. A theology, without a vital role for Mary as intermediary, is no theology at all to the Latin. If there is any chance at all of anyone getting what he wants that chance is best served by woman and since religion involves the deepest most important wishes one might have, it follows that Mary is the one who can bring this ultimate in fulfillment.

The woman, not so much as sex object but as covert and powerful authority figure, is the primary focus of Latin life and experience.

## For further reading

Nida, Eugene, "Mariology in Latin America", *Practical Anthropology,* Vol. 4, No. 3, 1957.

# *Chapter 13*

# *Activities*

### Calendar

Both Latin America and North America follow schedules based on the Gregorian Calendar of 365 days plus or minus. From this basic foundation, however, the calendar schedules diverge. The day schedule varies, the function of week, month and season cycles vary and the overall configuration of the year and multiyear scheduling differ.

There are at least two distinct day schedules operating in Latin America. They are both likely to begin and end at the same time but the configuration of the meal patterns are quite distinct. Five thirty to six thirty is the time range that the day begins. It ends around nine to ten except for weekends or holidays, which may extend until one or two o'clock in the morning.

One day schedule calls for a three meal pattern much like the North American pattern. Breakfast will be shortly after rising; lunch will be sometime during the noon siesta which runs from twelve until two, and dinner will be served around seven thirty in the evening. Within the bounds of this pattern, a light snack or coffee break will be served in the middle of the morning. The names given this sequence are *desayuno, almuerzo* and *comida*; or *desayuno, comida,* and *cena* with the snack called *refacción.*

The second dominant pattern will be a four meal day with coffee and sweet bread served in place of breakfast and a full meal called breakfast served at the hour of the snack; a lunch in the siesta period and dinner at about seven thirty. Even though the early meal is light, and more like a snack, it is perceived by the members of this subculture more as a meal than as a snack. It gets the day started, work can be accomplished and then one can sit down to a real breakfast after everything is underway.

As with all patterns, there can be variations on the theme. Other subcultures may have either the three or four meal sequence switching the main meal to the noon hour, but the main meal at night is the more dominant. The main meal at noon sequence is the one most dominant in the Philippines. As the North American who may have the evening meal dominant for the work week but will switch to the main meal at noon on Sunday, so will the Latin for certain occasions and on special days.

The work day begins early and ends late in relation to the North American schedule, primarily due to the siesta taken during the middle of the day. In urban areas certain sectors of the society are appearing to ignore the siesta but this is only a surface phenomenon. A given store will be kept open during the siesta but the number of staff will be lessened and the people in authority will not be there. It is not strange to find a given business open between seven thirty and eight in the morning, close at twelve or twelve thirty for siesta, reopen any time between two and three, and finally close at about six o'clock. A second pattern of business timing exists in certain areas where the proprietor of a business will spend whatever time he needs to, upon opening his business, to transact the business of the day and then close the establishment when he finishes. The business will remain closed until the following business day. Even where an establishment is not completely closed, the owner will leave and be on call. It is completely within reason to recall him to his office to transact business, even after he has left for the day. As we shall see in the section on values, it is not as important for the Latin to keep his establishment open just because of a time schedule if there is no further visible business to transact. He can be free to do other things that he chooses or that need to be done.

Many North Americans view the siesta as a nap. A nap to a North American is something that busy and important people just don't have time for, and even if they do they tend to excuse themselves by means of some rationalization. A nap is only for the sick or lazy. This judgment is quickly assigned to the Latin for various reasons which are quite logical to the North American but very demeaning to the Latin. The siesta is not so much a nap as a time for establishing family solidarity and reinforcing the sense of family and friendship. There is family fellowship at the time of siesta. It is incidental whether one naps or not. The nap is not the important thing. The significance lies in what it does for family. Friends may also be part of the siesta, sharing a meal in a local restaurant, eating in the home, or just being together. It does for the Latin family what the evening meal does for the North American family. It is the one time everyone is together and whether much is made of the experience or not, it is still important in the overall development of family.

## A LOOK AT LATIN AMERICAN LIFESTYLES

Even as the North American calendar schedule is associated with social and economic concerns such as the educational year, the vacation period, and the peaks of commercial enterprise—so the Latin calendar schedule is associated with religious traditions. Each day of the year has been assigned to a specific Catholic saint and depending upon a given saint's position in the hierarchy of saints, a certain importance is associated with the day. It is the combination of these days that produces the Latin calendar of events.

Lightly superimposed upon this sequence of days is the week, month and seasonal cycles which have to do more with the requirements of the church and preparing for festal occasions than with the beginning and ending of the economic work week, the payment of bills, the vacation period, etc. The week is designed to permit the citizen, and therefore church member, to worship once. The month schedule is not so much a bill paying time, but rather, a time for special events to happen and be taken care of in the life of the church, such as confession. The seasonal schedule is not tied so much to the educational scheduling that grew from the rural planting and harvesting arrangements, but more to the fertility cycle through the religious experience. Preparations are made for festivals, rather than school. School is incidental; the religious experience is focal.

The year and multiyear schedule has significance in terms of the church and its activities. The year highlights at Good Friday and all activities are done with Good Friday in focus, which is the peak of the festival cycle. Christmas and New Year are lesser days and thus lesser experiences. The year begins and ends with Good Friday, not New Year's day.

### Festival

The outsider, living in Latin America and ever aware of his surroundings, might react to the Latin life as one festival after another. Not everyone is involved in every festival, but there is an overall impression that all the Latin does is celebrate. There are probably more festival days in the Latin calendar than the North American one. There are more kinds of festivals, and the Latin tends to take his festivals more seriously than does the North American. Even as one is unable to ignore the church in Latin America it is impossible to be unaware of the festival cycle.

Each institution in Latin America has its own special festivals honoring some saint and thus has a birthday. The individual has his birthdate or saint's day. Each community has its own special day and the nation has its national holidays. Besides, the church has any number of festivals with Good Friday being the most significant in the festal cycle and such festivals as Corpus Cristi on the same level of importance as Christmas. The more significant the festival, the longer it is celebrated. Good Friday festival is a complex of festivals beginning with Lent and continuing after Easter. Christmas is another complex of festivals beginning December 6th and extending to Christmas Eve. It is quite distracting to the Protestant to discover a holiday unit ending prior to Easter and the day before Christmas with the people returning to their normal activities on these days when the Protestant holds these days as the most sacred. Various interpretations are given of this phenomenon such as, "they don't believe in the resurrection". The truth, however, lies closer to the established fact that they simply celebrate and remember Christ's death and resurrection over a distinct time span that may or may not have anything to do with what they believe about Christ and His resurrection. When one discounts the distinct, culturally established year schedules, it is possible to view objectively the distinctions of belief and faith. Once this is done one realizes that the Latin values Christ's resurrection equally with the North American.

In North America, preparation for festivals lies in selecting gifts and preparing meals, with a minimum of corporate activity such as preparation of the church building for the festival. The Latin turns a great deal of attention to the corporate processes. Religion to the Latin is more of a corporate and community activity and reinforcement than it is for the North American. The sanctuary and the edifice undergo the transformation for the festivals from special coverings on the floor to special decorations and colorful effects on walls and ceiling. The clothing of the saints receive special attention, either being washed or replaced. The clothing that adherents will wear receives special attention also, more like the Easter parade concept of the pre-World War Two period in North America. Whereas the Easter parade was limited to the Easter period primarily, the Latin pays this same attention to dress at each of the major festivals of the year. There will also be careful preparation of food made, but again the focus will be on the larger social group and will involve the extended family or the local community.

National and local community festivals are in some way directly or indirectly related to the church. The town festival is held, for example, on the saint's day assigned to the founding of the town. Even secular celebrations are subtle but powerful ties to the church.

## Life cycle

Many of the activities of the church revolve around life cycle crises and in this way link the church irrevocably with the developmental stages of maturation. There are four primary life crises, birth, puberty, marriage and death. It appears, examining the amount of ritual associated with the life crises and the intensity of feeling that attends the festival period, that death is the most significant of the rites of passage.

Certain societies, such as those with the couvade, i.e. the husband retiring to the bed upon the birth of the child and the wife taking up her normal activities, stress the birth rites of passage transitioning one from the world of the non-living to the world of the living. Other societies stress the birth period by a series of gift giving experiences. The Latin, generally, does not prepare for the child until the child is born. This is due in part to the high infant mortality rate. Whatever ritual is to attend the birth process follows birth, the most significant of these being baptism, usually administered within the first eleven days of the child's life, though it may be done as late as six months following birth. Throughout the ensuing period, since nothing is really sure about the potential for life of the child, the child is somewhat ignored and little more than baptism tends to focus the community's attention on the birth process. It is at birth and baptism that godparents are assigned the child.

Puberty becomes more visual with the rites of passage called confirmation and further assignment of godparents. However, since the primary season for assignment of godparents to a child is at birth, these godparents have more responsibilities to the child than do godparents at puberty and marriage. Confirmation then takes second priority to birth in importance. First communion may attend the ritual of confirmation. In some countries a coming out party is held for the child about the age of fifteen years.

Both life crises pale in importance to the marriage rites of passage. Marriage involves all the traditional preparations as chaperoned dating, arrangements and agreements involving intermediaries and spokesmen, formal points of progress such as engagement, preparations for the wedding, civil marriage and then church marriage with a large reception following. It is at this time that godparents are selected that function more significantly than do the godparents of confirmation though less than those of birth. Further, more visible preparations are made of food, drink, clothing, house decor, etc. More people will be involved both in preparation and participation and there will be a greater impact made on the community than at the two previous times.

Death is perhaps the most significant of the four life crises. The rites of passage that attend death are more elaborate in many ways and extend longer than do the rites of the other life crises. Immediately upon the death of an adult a wake is formed and preparations are made for the arrival of relatives and friends. Relatives and close friends are likely to arrive sooner and stay longer than is the case in North American society. There are greater limitations on the kind and amount of food that will be consumed than at marriage. There is always a procession that is attended by a large percentage of those at the funeral. The procession goes to the graveside and participates in a second ritual of death. A year following the death, there is another wake in memory of the departed. The restrictions on dress following death are more limiting than at the other rites as well. The color is black and the style is conservative. The widow may remain in mourning for as long as two years.

In the larger Latin community or society, puberty is not as significant a life crisis as it is in North America. The Latin lets the child go from childhood to adulthood without all the intervening rites of youth, teenage, graduations, evidences of maturation such as voting age, driver's license, etc. These are conceptually more compacted and a child, rather than moving into a teenage period with a fifth rite of passage called for, moves into a preadult period when there is the perception of adult, not of youth, and greater expectations are held by the elders in terms of the child's maturity.

Neither is retirement as significant to the Latin as it is to the North American. When the Latin is no longer able to do his job, he simply fades into obscurity. The North American focuses a bit more attention on this rite by assigning a status to retired people with economic and social visibility.

## For further reading

Bunzel, Ruth, *Chichicastenango,* University of Washington Press, Seattle, 1952.

Mangin, William, *Peasants in Cities,* Houghton Mifflin, 1970. Note especially Hans C. Buechler, "The Ritual Dimension of Rural-Urban Networks, The Fiesta System in the Northern Highlands of Bolivia".

# Chapter 14

# *Values*

Underlying all that a Latin is and does is a complex system of assigning values to qualities and actions. These qualities and actions are arranged in intricate priority rankings, the sum total of such patterning producing the Latin as distinct from the North American, the Portuguese, the Filipino, even the Spanish. One model that has been used to understand this system of valuing is to discuss social, economic, political and religious values. A second model is to consider the work ethic, the nature of faith, etc. Utilizing such models has produced interesting facts and statements regarding the Latin but they have done little to clarify the nature of interpersonal relationship that exists between the various members of the society, especially the subcultures. It is for this reason that I will work with a model designed to deal with the decision making process in the domain of interpersonal relations. The model is called basic values (Mayers 1974) and deals with twelve categories of motivation for action that derive from being, i.e. what one is. These categories include: event, time, dichotomy, holism, crisis, noncrisis, vulnerability as a strength or weakness, prestige as ascribed or assigned, interaction with person or goal. These are names assigned to existing patterns of behavior. No value judgments are assigned to the behavior pattern since description is intended.

### Event

The event oriented person is interested in who's there, what's going on, and how one can embellish the event with sound, color, light, body movement, touch, etc. He is less interested in time and schedule.

Perhaps the key concept for the North American to remember regarding the value orientation is that the Latin is more interested in the event than is the North American. There is a greater tendency to organize so that the event can be fulfilled, than to follow the time schedule. The Latin is not as event oriented as certain North American youth subcultures, or as the characteristic Indian cultures existing among the Latins. To the degree however, that the Latin is more concerned with person and embellished activity, to that degree he feels bound and restricted within the time structure of the North American.

The status system, operating in Latin America, calls for the person to be in focus. Thus, whenever one does something with others, it is important to know where each person is in relation to his own status. People knowing that a higher status person is or will be in their midst will do a variety of things to be present until that higher status person has left. It does not matter how long the higher status person delays in arriving or waits to leave, lower status people will remain and be basically content.

When people who are compatible in status and family organization are together, they wish to visit, which may very well be noisy even in a church setting. Protestant missionaries, from North America especially, decry the noise at the beginning of a worship service which to them calls for quiet. When the event is focused on, rather than the time schedule that calls for something to begin at a certain time and the participants ready to begin, there is less need for the so-called readiness. Event will follow event when people are ready, and not until. That which gives them a good feeling in being in the presence of others is that which is the best time for worship.

One of the key characteristics of the event oriented person is his desire to embellish the event. This is carried out in the Catholic church through the elaborate ritual, the body movement of the priest at the altar, and the color of the altar. The Pentecostals attained significant growth in South America largely due to embellishing the event with tongues and healing. These practices have served to bring the community of believers together and to give them the good feeling essential to the event person. Without this good feeling he does not know if something worthwhile has happened or not. The Protestant tends to focus on his message and has ruled out the good feeling as an emotional response—the Gospel not needing any emotional response, but rather a thought-through decision to follow Christ.

The sharp focus on the person, and the action involving person with the attempts to embellish the event leads the society toward an existentialism or nowness less characteristic of the North American society. This results in greater spontaneity with lack of structure characterizing such spontaneity. Thus, a deadline may already be

# A LOOK AT LATIN AMERICAN LIFESTYLES

contracted in the event an opportunity, previously unconsidered, arises. If the opportunity is such that it appeals to the Latin more than the completion of the contract, he will move the contracted time back and take his opportunity. He can do this without any qualms of conscience that might arise from his unilateral change of contract. The opportunity he has is worth more than a time schedule. This idea is reflected in the language where the definite future tense is used much less than the subjunctive ("doubtful" mood). They feel that one might be so occupied planning and saving for the future (which indeed may never come) that he misses the joys of the present.

Parades, processions, floral decorations, and corporately designed flower petal decorations in the streets all attest to the event oriented nature of the Latin. His love for the embellished event far outweighs his concern for a time schedule.

## Time

The Latin's focus on the event and the event fulfilled does not mean he is totally unaware of time and the clock to the degree that some North Americans are led to believe. They associate a certain laziness to the Latin stereotyped by the Mexican sitting and leaning against a wall with his sombrero down over his face. The Latin is not lazy, but rather is quite active within his own conceptualization of time and sequence schedule.

The time oriented person is concerned with the time period: when it begins, when it ends, how long it takes. There will be concern for the range of punctuality, i.e. how long it takes to get started or end. The time period will be carefully planned in order to get everything done. This will result in the concept of proper length.

For the North America, the event tends to be dominated by the time schedule. For the Latin American there is a tendency to let the event come to fulfillment more naturally, though he does pay attention to the time. He knows when something is to start, but he knows better when something he wants to be involved in starts. He manages to be where he really wants to be, to be with people he wishes to be with. This in itself causes a certain amount of attention to the time schedule.

He knows just how long he can delay in keeping with the status relationship of the person he is meeting, or the meeting he is attending. This range of punctuality is a key factor in the Latin experience. It is perhaps the most significant timing device of the Latin. Every action, every relationship has its own range of punctuality. The higher the status of the person or group, the narrower the range of punctuality. An appointment with the president of the nation requires that one be there not one second early and not one second late. The lower the status of the individual, the greater the range of punctuality. A householder's appointment with an applicant can be delayed a couple of hours without either party needing an excuse. One cannot be late for mass without feeling affected, but one can arrive within the first half hour of a meeting in a Protestant church service without feeling late. The business event demands a narrower range than does the social event. Finally, the larger the size of an item purchased, repaired or replaced, the broader the range of punctuality. An iron may be promised for a week from the time of agreement by a repairman and not returned for three weeks. A refrigerator will be promised two to four weeks from time of agreement but be actually delivered up to two to three months from that time. The reason given is difficulty in securing parts, but experience quickly shows that is is more than parts, since all items tend to receive the same basic treatment.

The past is also very important as something accomplished, or something one can be sure about. So you will find that they celebrate dates to be remembered to a greater extent than we do and with more ceremony: the anniversary of some battle, the birth or death of some personage. Since scientific development has been more rapid in North America, something that is perhaps two years old is considered quite old and out of date. But in South America the past is not seen as so remote, perhaps because there is more effort to keep it alive.

The Latin American has been more prone to accept customs and traditions without question and so without an urge to try to change them. This is still true to a great extent, especially in very conservative areas (outside of the large centers and even in cities like Arequipa and Ayacucho) and especially among humble folk. Even though in this generation free thinking has come into its own and students especially are questioning everything, what we see of Latin American culture today is permeated with custom and tradition. They feel their social and religious obligations keenly. The North American is not free of custom and tradition, fortunately, for there is a certain beauty in it. But it does not affect every area of life as greatly as it does in Latin America, where an adequate and acceptable explanation for something might be *es costumbre* "it is the custom".

## Holism

The holist will view life as one whole and may or may not concern himself with the parts. Whenever parts are considered they must be in relation to the whole. Situations demanding consideration of parts without the perspective of the whole become frustrating.

The Latin tends to start from the whole to view the making up the whole. To be Latin is to be Catholic. To be living in Guatemala is to be

# A LOOK AT LATIN AMERICAN LIFESTYLES

Guatemalan. To be part of family is to be whole family. There will be distinctions of family and family, of nation and nation, but these will come after the conceptualization of the whole. This is what makes border disputes so difficult for the North American to comprehend, in that the nation claiming a piece of land now belonging to a second nation still considers it an integral part of their nation. The cry *Belice es nuestro* means far more than "it belongs to us" to the Guatemalan. It means that it was, is now, and always will be an integral part of Guatemala. It is part of the total destiny of the nation. It is to be included in all maps, in all thoughts. If, in fact, someone distinguishes it as other than Guatemala, that person is persona non grata to the Guatemalan. Being is never dichotomized as far as the Latin is concerned.

## Dichotomism

The dichotomist will tend to divide the whole into parts and tend to be more concerned with the parts than with the whole. This leads him to consider a part as the whole, to ignore the other parts of the whole. Part or parts become the ultimate existence and such intense focus on parts produces sharpness of definition of the part.

Once being is established as whole, behavior can proceed in relation to the parts. Everyone must discern those Latin and those not Latin. Everyone must behave one way toward those higher in status and a different way toward those lower in status. One is either Catholic or a nobody. One is a parent or coparent. One is part of family or not part of family. One functions or does not function within the society.

## Person

The person is the primary focus of life with all goals, purposes and achievements revolving around person. Something done is meaningless unless there is person to do or to receive. Person is thing unless known and related to other person in some dynamic way.

Person related to person is of high value in Latin society. A gift without relationship is meaningless. A thing or object cannot stand in the way of relationship. If a friend asks for a possession, it is nearly impossible for the Latin to refuse him. The Spanish phrase *asi es su casa* or "my house is yours" is more than just a nice way of expressing friendship. It strikes at the very heart of possession to the Latin. Nothing that the Latin has is apart from relationship. The relationship controls, not the object. Once this is established, the rules of possession assign land to family and provide the protocol to enable family to retain possessions. But irrespective of such rules, possession must fulfill relationship and where it does, life is meaningful and there is security.

Person is only meaningful in family context. The matrix of family formed by the intersection of the axes of nuclear and extended family is of significance and deep meaning to the Latin. Person is only an entity within the intersection of columns and rows of family involvement. It is here that he receives his primary socialization, that which is to dominate his life forever. The Latin in North America will form relationships as similar as possible to those of his early experience. This is not lost for generations, if it ever is lost.

The seeming impersonalness of the North American and his perceived concern for object for object's sake tends to frustrate the Latin.

### Prestige is ascribed

The person who feels that prestige is ascribed and then confirmed by the society makes every effort to know his prestige in relation to others, to maintain that level of prestige, and to make sure that he has the qualities that reflect his prestige. No sacrifice is too great to maintain his status or to rise in status if this reinforces his own prestige.

Within the context of Spanish and thus Latin life, every person enters life on a distinct status level and this standing in the community must be maintained at all costs and improved in any way possible. Prestige is thus assigned to the Latin as role, rather than Latin as an individual entity. In comparison, the North American, whatever the elements are within the society that operate in terms of ascription of prestige (whoever is elected president has all the prestige accorded that office the moment he is inaugurated), is very much a prestige achieved person. He assumes he must make it himself and everyone about him must make it also. The Latin always has it. He does not have to make it though he must improve it if possible. The greatest degradation possible for the Latin is to lose his standing in relation to others. His prestige is correlated with his status level.

### Vulnerability is a weakness rather than a strength

The person who feels that vulnerability is a weakness will do everything in his power to avoid the perception of error, weakness, mistake.

All of Latin society is designed to support the person so he does not err, and to cover for the person who does. The language reflects, quite accurately, this desire to prove to the outside world that the Latin is errorless. The phrase *se perdió* "it lost itself" is a type of response that places the blame for error on the object, not on the person whose loss it was.

A family unable to meet certain financial obligations will go to other members of the family and they are in turn obligated to respond favorably so as to maintain the perception of financial stability. A politician, losing an election, will do a number of things to maintain office and, barring that, will retire into seclusion for a lengthy period of time until it is forgotten, or at least appears to be forgotten. A person reprimanded in public will seek vengeance and even if death or destruction results, he will be exonerated by the community since he had reason to do what he did. A person who refuses to honor a contract or agreement, after it has been formally or informally announced, effects a deeply felt personal affront to the persons involved, e.g. the person who agrees to become a coparent or who is perceived to be interested, and then declines is seen as an ingrate to the Latins involved.

Interpersonal relations that preserve the errorlessness of the participants are therefore to be maintained. One of the mechanisms of society to insure this perception is that of intermediary. The intermediary serves so that one participant in a relationship will not have to say no directly to the other and thus break that relationship.

## Crisis

The person who is crisis oriented operates in terms of high definition of alternative, i.e. one possibility only is in focus; high definition of authority, i.e. every situation or challenge has the authority of resolution; and an enduring sense of proof lying in the historical process.

Latin society has a tendency to present one alternative and stand by that alternative. One is born into a status level; a child losing his parents cannot possibly merge within another family on the same basis as natural children; one person has power-legislating against a two party political system; one is Catholic or nothing at all.

Latin society has an authority established for every function within the society. This is high definition authority to whom everyone responsible must relate. The father is the authority in the home; the head of the extended family is the authority beyond the home; the president is the authority in the nation. The decree of any is to be followed unquestioningly, though in fact it might not be. The church is the highest authority, even over nation. The nation is the authority over all that is other than church, etc.

History becomes the validating process for all authority. The Latin is therefore very traditional in the sense that what was done in the past becomes a standard for the present and future. Growing out of this sense of history is a fatalism that influences every aspect of life, expressed in *Dios voluntad,* or "the will of God", which makes whatever happens right.

## For further reading

Mayers, Marvin K., *Christianity Confronts Culture,* Zondervan, Grand Rapids, 1974.

# Chapter 15

# The Economic Life

The Latin American is primarily oriented to the product from the land, not to the land itself, nor to any kind of specific system of production or distribution. The Indian person living in the area of Latin involvement is more likely to be oriented to the land itself and his ability to make the land produce. The North American is more concerned with systems of production and distribution and in his dealings with the Latin attempts to impose such a system upon him. The Latin resists working with his hands and he resists the perceived oversystematization that comes from the North American recommendations.

The marriage of convenience that results from the distinct work orientation of Latin and Indian brings the two together in a program of production that lets the Indian be fulfilled as he sees the land produce, and lets the Latin be fulfilled as he can dispose of the products of the land for his own ends. Such marriage often ends in abuse with the Indian receiving low wages in relation to the overall income of the Latin and also in the restricted mobility imposed upon the Indian. He is unable to rise in status and is further limited in his opportunity to seek new employment elsewhere. The Indian is not a slave. Rather he is a freeman whose horizons are limited both by the system and by his association with Latins.

The machinery established to have the land produce to the benefit of the Latin is the *patrón-mozo* relationship. There is a landowner or supervisor who hires *mozos* or helpers. The *mozo* may be hired by the day but more than likely he will become established on a piece of the land he is to work and be able to call that his own (about three-fourths of an acre), be entitled to a certain amount of staples each month (about a hundred pounds of grain or corn), receive wages for at least two weeks of work (anywhere from thirty-five cents to two dollars or equivalent per day), and expect certain social and health services as educational and work opportunities for his children and medical care in times of illness. In most areas of Latin America where Indian people live in close proximity to the Latin, the Indian fills the role of *mozo* and the Latin as owner or supervisor. Where there are no Indian people or where the supply is insufficient for the needs of the landowner, other Latins will be hired.

The landowner or rancher is the boss who rules his property much as a dictator. Many such owners are benevolent and the supervision they provide for their employees is greatly beneficial to them. It is not the responsibility of the central government to provide social and health services, rather of the landowner. In most areas of Latin America, there is no specific law that has decreed this. Anything that is done for the benefit of the *mozo* or hired hand is likely all that will be done for him and in most cases is appreciated. The unscrupulous landowner, however, can make the *mozo's* life miserable. One such way is to open a *cantina,* or a stall serving alcoholic beverages, at the location where the *mozos* are paid. Frequently, the *mozos* get so drunk that they spend all their wages on the alcohol they are consuming or lose whatever is left in the process of getting home. It is not uncommon for the wives of such men to approach the paymaster's desk with the husband and take immediate control of the wages. The Indian, seeking employment away from his home area is highly susceptible to such tricks and will frequently return home in greater debt than he left.

Even apart from the full-time *mozo* relationship, any part-time employment is likely to be effected with a *patrón* supervising a *mozo*. The North American assumes that he is hiring a man to do the work he has available and discovers on the day appointed that the man he hired is the supervisor of another man or men who will actually do the job.

One of the problems that plagues the North American working within Latin America is that the Latin expects the *patrón* to provide all the benefits that are called for in wage, land, and services. The North American approaches hiring from the standpoint of wages alone and literally refuses to provide other than that which is part of the North American hiring scene. Other agencies educate and provide medical assistance and every employee is expected to find their own housing and pay for it out of their wages. This produces the phenomenon of the "partial *patrón-mozo* relationship." It is expressed in such hiring relationships as the day laborer, dealing with a beggar who is seeking not so much a meal as a *patrón,* or in the hiring of church employees in the Protestant church. The Protestant mission program, built on the culture of North America, trains and hires a pastor much as one would be hired in the States. Demands for housing are quickly taken care of with little additional cost, because the pastor can live in one of the rooms of the church structure. The services are more difficult to come by, however, for the mission will assume they will be taken care of by the immediate employer, i.e. the Protestant mission organization.

## Residence patterns

Residence patterns growing out of the *patrón-mozo* relationship are, generally speaking, the *patrón* living in a prominent place on his land and the *mozos* living in less choice spots on the land or near the land where the land arrangement is not part of their contract. The latter sets up villages proximate to the land available for farming. These villages will generally be only houses but if the secular or religious officials recognize the village as of some importance, a public house will be constructed to house secular officials, a church will be constructed and, in time, a rural market can be established. Towns are villages raised in status in this way and cities are towns that have grown due to their strategic location or industry.

## Multicrop harvest

The planting season in Latin America depends on the particular crop or the altitude at which it is being planted. Since the land configuration of Latin America involves the mountain yielding to the valley, with large percentages of the land surface on the mountainside, there is great variation of crop and altitude. One man can plant a corn crop on the mountainside as high as it will grow, a second crop on the mountainside at some lower altitude and a third crop in a valley and have three crops in this way rather than one. He is thus potentially occupied for a longer period of time than he would be with land at one specific altitude. He might also have a garden of squash, or even a vine or two of a similar product. These could be growing at times when there are no other crops growing. Whereas in the valley or on the coast there is one time to plant and one time to harvest, in the average mountain area there is something being planted and harvested throughout the year.

Famine is therefore not a time when there is nothing to eat as much as a time when there are no staples. When there is no corn or wheat or yucca, then there is famine. Famine relief is the provision of corn in a corn eating area, or wheat in a wheat eating area.

## The rural market

The rural market is held in a village or town from one to five days a week. People attend the market to sell and buy. The more rural the market the more stress is placed on selling before one can buy. The more urban the rural market, for each urban center has at least one such market, the greater the distinction of seller and buyer. Each community has its own market day or days and some vendors make their living from moving from one to another, selling their produce, buying what is characteristic of that town and returning to their own to sell this in turn.

The rural market functions primarily as a social institution and only secondarily as an economic institution. The people are there to be with people, rather than to make money. There will be numerous social gatherings attending the rural market from the repeated encounter of two women sitting side by side who only see each other at this time to a group of men spending an entire day at the stockpens while they make arrangements for sales of animals. Women encountered going to market will seldom sell along the way and never sell all their produce, even though they know they might not sell it all at the market. Were they to sell all their produce they would have no reason to go and this would be tragic.

Bargaining has become a way of life throughout Latin America. The bargaining process involves the buyer who has decided he might buy some product and the seller who has this product to sell. The buyer will ask the price and the seller will respond with an inflated price, higher for the stranger and lower for the friend. The buyer is then expected to offer a reduced price, lower than the price he wishes to pay. This process continues until a price is decided upon by mutual agreement, when one or the other meets the price stated. The bargaining process is a social encounter. It not only consumes time, it makes life exciting. The North American feels it is a waste of time, that they are taking advantage of the seller (or vice versa), that there is something unpleasant in the experience. The Latin on the other hand not only enjoys the social interaction but can also use this process to judge the character of the person met in a social encounter. Some vendors will refuse to sell to those people they have discovered to be unworthy of respect, even people of higher status whom the vendor cannot respect. The tougher the bargain struck, the higher regard the vendor has for the buyer. This is not important in terms of the direct social encounter of buyer and seller for, depending upon their respective status levels, they are not likely to meet outside the market for social intercourse. It is important, however, for building the reputation of the person in the community for this information is known in ever widening circles as the years, decades and genera-

# A LOOK AT LATIN AMERICAN LIFESTYLES

tions pass. The more the vendor respects the buyer, the more likelihood there will be of fixing a fair price on the object when the respected buyer approaches.

The economic functions of the market involve not only the provision for the local residents but the distribution of goods throughout the entire country. Middlemen go to a given market and carry produce from that market to larger centers where it is collected and retransported. This is being done, however, in conjunction with the social aspects of market. Any ignoring of the social proprieties of the market limit the opportunity to purchase the products in quantities that are desired.

The market place also serves as a haven for abandoned women. The woman who has been a mistress and now becomes a public ward frequently will live in a market stall as guard until she is taken in by another man as his mistress. These women may become prostitutes and remain such throughout the rest of their lives. Often, they are part of a pool of available women from which some men will choose a wife and some a mistress.

Each urban center will have at least one rural market where the roles are more distinctly identified as seller or buyer but little of the flavor of the rural market is lost. Some urban officials, attempting to contain the market, will construct a large market edifice and impose a head tax on the vendors. They will do this to get the rural market participants off the city streets. If the building is too confining or the head tax too steep, the vendors will flow out into the streets again and resist all efforts at containment.

## Penny capitalism

Sol Tax, writing about the Indian socioeconomic system of Panajachel, Guatemala talks about the penny base for trade and barter. Whereas the dollar has become a standard for an industrialized society, the penny is the monetary standard for the preindustrialized society. Rural Latin America is more influenced by the penny than by the dollar. The thought of cost in dollars to the penny capitalist is like the thought of cost in millions of dollars to the dollar capitalist. It simply blows one's mind. That which is undertaken receives "grass roots" support if the costs are in the pennies, dollars and tens of dollars. If they are in the hundreds or thousands of dollars, the plan is resisted.

This is not to say that the Latin is unable to handle larger sums. Rather, the Latin will handle larger sums much like he handles the smaller sums. Whatever amount of money he has is probably not deposited in a bank. Cash may go into a buried urn or into land purchase rather than into a bank or a savings and loan or a stock or bond program. Insurance lies with the extended family and ties of reciprocity and loyalty rather than with an insurance, investment or retirement program. It is further expected that no one will have large sums of available cash, but that all the nuclear families together within an extended family can come up with all that is needed at a given point in time.

Time payments, credit terms and mortgages are all relatively incomprehensible to the rural Latin. It has only been with the industrialization and growing urbanization that such money mechanisms have begun to gain acceptance with the Latin. Even now, there is a built-in distrust for any money organization, and these are approached only as a last resort. It is not uncommon for the manager of a financial fund to use the actual money for developing reciprocal relations that will enhance his own status position in the society. One of the roles assigned to the North American in a Latin organization, e.g. church association, is that of banker since the Latin says, "We can trust you." What they mean is that they can trust the North American not to use the funds for prestige enhancement. It does not mean that the Latin is untrustworthy.

With a bare subsistence and minimum money base, there is not the constant, ongoing expenditure of funds found in North American society where affluence has made funds available for rather constant small cost purchases. In Latin America the festival provides the opportunity for money expenditure either for religious reasons or for dress. Religious purposes may include ceremonial costs such as for a special mass, or for the alcoholic beverage that accompanies the celebration. Drinking practices during festivals drain financial resources and leave many Latins in debt or with an extensive hangover. The Indian does not have the latter problem quite as much since he is a festival drunk. He is likely to be drunk during the festival and sober the moment it is over.

## Service responsibility

Certain functions of civil government, as messenger, warrior, etc. are hired out in North America on a non-quota basis, but are part of the responsibility of the average citizen in Latin America. The Latin can be called upon at any time during his adult life to fill such functions. He must serve personally or provide a replacement. He is not likely to be called upon twice for the same service obligation though this is not outside the realm of possibility. The process of selection and service is much like the selection of jurors in the United States. However, there are some selections and appointments to service obligations made when some high ranking official is seeking revenge on another.

## A LOOK AT LATIN AMERICAN LIFESTYLES

The local government does not need the same corporate funding as does the North American community. The tax equivalent distributes corporate responsibilities throughout the community as for example the educational responsibility being laid at the door of the *patrón* and the community services operations being staffed by volunteers.

### Tipping

In North American society, the tipping practice is generally the post-tip, i.e. the tip is given in keeping with services rendered. Thus a person will get a haircut and tip the barber, or order a meal and tip the waitress. To the North American, the pre-tip is seen as a bribe, the indication being that you will receive financial remuneration if and when you comply with my wishes even though that which I want is extra legal. The Latin, on the other hand, makes use of the pre-tip for numerous services calling for the post-tip in North America or no tip. The local neighborhood guard is paid for his services through the pre-tip, the indication that I am glad you are around and would you kindly watch my property as you are watching others. The border official is encouraged to give good service to the traveller by means of the pre-tip. Such practices are perceived by North Americans as bribes and a decision must be made as to whether to participate or not. No such decision is made in tipping the waitress though it is whenever a pre-tip is called for. The pre-tip is easily distinguished from the bribe in that the bribe is assigned whenever there is a law on the books. For example, every driver of a vehicle must have a medical checkup prior to receiving a driver's license. A large corporation may provide the medical examiner's office with a case of liquor prior to the examination of its chauffeurs, not for better service in handling their applications, but so they will not have to take the examination at all. In many offices, where the pre-tip is called for in the legal sense, a receipt may be extended to indicate the amount of the tip.

### Industry

With the introduction of the industrial complex and the increasing urbanization, many socioeconomic practices are undergoing change. Whatever develops is still based on the above mentioned principles, making Latin industry truly Latin.

### For further reading

Friedrich, Paul, *Agrarian Revolt in a Mexican Village,* Prentice-Hall, Englewood Cliffs, N.J., 1970.

Morris, James O., *Elites, Intellectuals and Concensus,* New York State School of Industrial and Labor Relations, Cornell University, Ithaca, N.Y., 1966.

Nash, Manning, *Machine Age Maya,* American Anthropological Association, Memoir 87, 1958.

Tax, Sol, *Penny Capitalism,* Smithsonian Institution, Institute of Social Anthropology Publication 16, 1963.

Wolf, Eric, *Sons of the Shaking Earth,* University of Chicago Press, Chicago, 1959.

# Chapter 16

# The Changing Scene in Latin America

There is no part of Latin America which is untouched by change. In some sectors the change is drastic, in others not as drastic. In some aspects of life the change reaches to the very foundations of the society, in others the change is superficial. In such a great continent as South America where there is great divergence of life styles, and there are many problems unique to Spanish background societies, change is both inevitable and irreversible. In all the developments, whatever the cataclysm, the result will still be Latin, reflecting the Spanish or Portuguese backgrounds. However similar a house style will be to a North American one, the handling of the house, its purchase, decoration and resale will be Latin in pattern. The living done within it will still be oriented to the relatives and ritual relatives far more than will the North American counterpart.

## Population growth in Latin America

The population growth of Latin America is greater than in North America. If present rates of increase continue, Latin America will have twice as many people as the United States by the end of this century. Mexico has the fastest growing population in the world.

## Changes in social structure

One of the key factors in affecting change in social structure is the disappearance of the Indian population. Two forces are at work to reduce the Indian population—the natural dying out of Indian groups and the systematic, planned elimination of the Indian people. The first process is the slower of the two for with every loss of an Indian group, there has been the resurgence of another. One of the principal reasons for the decimation of the Indian population by natural means has been the introduction of diseases from the outside world for which the Indian has not developed a natural immunity. The second process proceeds quite rapidly either by physical force or social pressure to assimilation within the Latin society.

As the Indian populations disappear or assimilate to Latin lifeways, the caste system, defined by Tumin will also disappear. However much the Latin feels constrained to assent to its demise, and however much the outside world would rejoice that his lingering barrier to social equality would be eliminated, the caste system provides a number of benefits to the total society which need to be replaced with functional equivalents so that the benefits will not be lost. One of these benefits is allowing the Indian population to fulfill its own identity and destiny. However much abused the Indian populations are they can still maintain their Indianness in Latin America and do this within a favored environment. Conflict only comes when the two groups meet.

Emerging middle class consciousness is producing the "middle groups". Within the strata rank system operating in Latin America, a person is conceptually on his own strata level and no one else is on that same level. For the sake of supporting the individual who would otherwise be a total isolate in every respect, the society allows his nuclear family as well as his associating extended family to share his same level perceptually. What this has meant, especially in rural areas, is that it has been difficult, if not impossible, to group people together for any function in other than family groups. With the emergence of a middle class mentality, it is now possible, in urban centers especially, to get people together who view themselves as the same. This is producing not one middle class, but middle groups. A given group will associate with others not related to them by family, but sharing common goals, hopes and aspirations. A given group will not necessarily associate with another given group. However, all the middle groups can become influenced by middle class propaganda from the mass media. To refer to the metaphor of the status ladder, instead of the ladder bulging at one point, i.e. the middle zone of the ladder, it has numerous bulges throughout the middle of the ladder.

Associated with this emergence of the middle groups is a developing urban proletariat with independent political power. Whereas previously, political power resided in the upper statuses, increasingly the middle groups are negating this power and reshaping it to their ends. As the process continues, and family name yields to wealth as a primary means of upward mobility, there is a developing moneyed upper class to replace the old rich.

Also associated with the emergence of the middle groups is a development of trade unions. The freeing of power to move down the status ladder releases a variety of interest groups to struggle anew for identity. These trade unions are attempting to effect a reciprocal relationship between boss and employee to replace the unidirectional decision making process that formerly existed to the benefit of the landed and wealthy and the detriment of the laboring man. There had formerly been unions of craftsmen who joined together for the sake of their craft. The new unions are not so much oriented to the development of the craft as they are to the betterment of working conditions for the laborer within the craft.

The decline of illiteracy is also effecting changes in the social structure. Previously, in many areas of Latin America, there had been as high as 93 to 95 percent illiteracy. Such lack of preparedness to interact in the larger community and national interests reduced the pool of leaders to a select few. With the growing literacy, the pool of leaders broadens and privilege is extended. The subtle influences on Latin life such as a covert support of increasing industrialization and the willingness to sacrifice to ultimately achieve its benefits are constantly being felt. Fidel Castro, of Cuba, though repudiated by most governments of the Western hemisphere, has been accomplishing something significant in reducing illiteracy and has challenged other Latin governments to do the same.

## Emancipation of women

Traditionally the woman in Latin America has had to be content to exercise her real authority quite covertly, beginning in the home with little chance of it being carried farther except indirectly through her offspring. As more and more women entered secretarial and teaching positions the horizon opened for them to extend their influence beyond the home. Today it is not surprising to find women doctors, women mayors and women serving in other occupations and professions formerly seen as for men only. San Juan, Puerto Rico; Santiago, Chile; and Caracas, Venezuela have all had women mayors in recent decades.

## Economic change in Latin America

With the emergence of the middle groups, there is a redistribution of income thus putting more money into the pockets of these sectors and making it available for consumer type purchases. This redistribution of funds has both encouraged the developing middle class mentality and has also reinforced strands of the development from other sources.

With the need for more consumer goods, host countries have become partners in internal developments by outside firms. Such partnerships do not come without problems, the ultimate being the nationalization of the industry and the dispossession of the partner by the host nation. There are many advantages, however, that more than make up for such a risk even if the risk becomes realized. Such benefits are centered around an increase of available monies in terms of loans, and capital investments as well as the circulation of more actual cash rewards.

As industry enters Latin America it is quickly realized that a given country cannot possibly support all the industry it needs. Thus a common market begins to form, much as that in Central America, where agreement is reached as to which countries will provide which goods so that no two countries will provide the same goods and thus duplicate effort needlessly. The unity sought on a political level decades and centuries ago may at last become realized in the economic sphere.

Within the common market, tariff regulations favor industry within and discourage it from without. Such regulations make possible the development of heavy industry which can now be made available in a broader socioeconomic sector than was previously possible. The larger the sphere of tariff regulation, the heavier the industry that is possible.

The heavier the industry permitted in a socioeconomic sector, the more likelihood there is that farm equipment will replace men in the fields. The mountainous terrain legislates against this happening to the degree it has in North America, but there are areas of Brazil and Argentina where machinery is totally revolutionizing farming. The factories then draw the men from the fields to the urban areas and the social and economic changes mentioned previously accelerate. Electricity also extends into the rural areas to change patterns of life including the day schedule and the continued shift from farm to light industry.

Throughout the entire process of shift from an agricultural to an industrial economy, the gradual program of land reform continues. It moves faster during certain periods, but overall is simply a process showing progress that is steady, but not spectacular. The institution of the church tends to slow the process as well as do the vested interests of the upper statuses.

## Religious change

Active participation of laymen in the church, in many traditional respects, has been on the decline. This sounds strange when one hears of revolutionary new programs of aggressive laymen in the church. What is happening, is a disenchantment with the church in its traditional forms. The revolution within the church is designed to win back those who have been lost and get the laymen actively engaged once again.

One of the means the church has utilized in attracting the laymen is to permit the clergy to dress more in the layman's street garb, rather than the religious habit. Many religious orders in Latin America permit lay garb all the time or at least at strategic times. One of the significant breakthroughs has come with the adoption of street dress by certain religious orders of nuns.

The Protestant church has been accepted in many sections of Latin America as church rather than sect. The term of reference has been "men of goodwill" and the behavior has been that of accepting Protestants as equals whereas groups such as B'ahai and the Mormons are reacted to as sect or non-church. This attitude has opened many doors previously inaccessible to Protestants. One of the Protestant organizations most readily received on a partnership basis in Latin America is the Summer Institute of Linguistics. Wherever they are working they are in some cooperative relationship with the national government seeking to aid the ethnic populations within the larger society.

The particular branch of Protestantism enjoying the most rapid growth in Latin America, especially in South America, is the pentecostal. Growth rates in certain countries, such as Chile, have been phenomenal. The type of experience of the pentecostal is apparently attractive to the Latin insofar as initial attention and conversion to Protestantism is concerned. Maturing Christians who wish to do more intense Bible and theological study turn to other branches of Protestantism.

Overall, within the religious experience, there is a growing secularization. This was, perhaps, most marked after the turn of the century in Mexico, but has continued with increasing intensity to the present day. The result is a weakening hold of the traditional church on all aspects of Latin life. Prior to the turn of the century, the religious influence permeated and controlled all other aspects of life. Today this is true in only the most rural and undeveloped areas of Latin America. To be religious is to be Catholic or Protestant; to be Latin is to be Latin. No longer can it be said that to be Latin is to be either Catholic or religious. Religion is not dead, and at times the sacred forces will appear to dominate, but they are unable to consolidate control and to exercise power over the masses in the way they have in the past.

## For further reading

Adams, Richard N., et al, *Social Change in Latin America Today*, Vintage Books, N.Y., 1960.

Horowitz, Irving Louis, *Masses in Latin America,* Oxford University Press, N.Y., 1970.
Johnson, John J., *Continuity and Change in Latin America,* Stanford University Press, Stanford, 1964.
Senior, Clarence, *The Puerto Ricans,* Quadrangle Books, Chicago, 1965.
Veliz, Claudio, ed., *Obstacles to Change in Latin America,* Oxford University Press, London, 1969.
Wagner, Nathaniel H., and Marsha J. Haug, *Chicanos,* C. V. Mosby, St. Louis, 1971.

# Chapter 17

# The Agent of Change

The educator, the businessman, the government worker, the missionary, the minister, and the marriage counsellor become agents of change at least for a portion of his stay in Latin America. He seeks to change that which he finds because it does not coincide with that which he has found to work for himself and because he senses that not all of Latin society works for the benefit of the Latin insofar as the Latin himself is concerned. As he gets to work, he finds the Latin encouraging him. As the Latin, seeking change, discovers support from the change agent, he not only becomes encouraged but he becomes a loyal friend of the change agent.

The ultimate test of the change agent, however, is not so much his decision to do something, with or without the Latin in consultation, but rather, the people responding, "We are glad you came". The opposite cry is one of nationalism, a message that indicates one's stay is not at all appreciated. "Yankee, go home" has been one of the overt expressions of this message, one that tells the outsider that he has blown it insofar as his ultimate purpose is concerned.

The agent of change can work directly, thoroughly and in great depth and receive the accolade, "We want you here, we want you to stay". How does one go about accomplishing his purpose and eliciting such a positive response?

**Live up to status expectations**

Status and prestige rank is so important to the Latin that anyone dealing with him must pay attention to the various aspects of status. The change agent is likely to enter Latin America as a high status person.

This means he needs to pay attention to the behavior expected of him so that he might maintain this level; pay attention to the behavior evidenced in the other so that the other can maintain, if not improve his standing in the community; and finally do those things that reinforce the status levels and the expectations of both within the society. The change agent cannot live up to his own status level if he is continually undermining the status level of the other. Neither can he build and maintain a trust relationship with the Latin if he is forever denigrating his own status level. This puts everyone associating with him on edge since it calls their own prestige rating into serious question.

It is further important that the change agent move from status to status in the influence and decision making process. When the higher status person moves into Latin America and associates only with the lower status people two kinds of reactions are forthcoming. The upper status people lose confidence in him because he is not living up to his status and thus is perceived as irresponsible. Lower status people distrust both his person and his purpose since they hold open the question, "Why is he associating with us?"

There are ways of effecting influence from status level to status level. The first principle to follow is to make and maintain high status contacts and friendships. Secondly, even if one is to move into the lower status groupings, he needs to move in and out, returning to his higher status associations sufficiently to maintain the perception of his high standing. The third principle is that he develop his organization so that he will have working under him and with him those who are potential for relating with each level of status. One member of his organization will work with the status levels directly below his own. Other workers will be involved with other levels (whether formal or informal) that will build the trust and confidence of each strata level. Finally, the change agent must be sure that his own friendships and contacts and all activities of his organization work for the developing trust in relationship. For example, if uninterrupted or smooth reading is an expectation of the higher status person, that person will not read in public. He will have a subordinate read. This will accomplish a number of things. If he were to read publicly and stumble, the perception of his status would be lowered. The subordinate automatically reinforces the higher status person's higher standing. This is reinforced especially if the subordinate himself stumbles in his reading, i.e. "the superordinate can read and never make a mistake". The hearer will think this whether he ever heard the superordinate read or not. Finally, the subordinate becomes related integrally with the higher status person in the minds of the people.

The change agent also needs to pay attention to the principle of upward mobility. This simply suggests that there is an inborn and integral urging within every Latin to rise in status. This is not "keeping up with the Joneses" type of thing, rather a fulfillment of human potential type. Anyone who can help the Latin rise in social standing not only has his loyalty, but also will be constantly aware of his appreciation. Simply by associating with a lower status person, the higher status person helps him. Any further effort on the part of the higher status person to effect a rise in status for the lower status person adds to the benefits. Arranging marriage for such a person is helpful so long as one rises in status. Arranging for a job or an opening in a profession is a help. Admitting a person into a school which aids him in his upward mobility is of great benefit.

Care must be taken in working with the Latin that no undue pressure is placed upon the one rising in status to jump statuses. If he rises too far too fast he is not only mistrusted by those he has displaced on the status ladder, but his personal tensions increase as he struggles to work out the details of the new and demanding expectations of the higher status. Many well meaning organizations move a Latin too far too quickly and the Latin's inconsistent behavior undermines the confidence of his employers, something that need not come about since the Latin intends responsibility.

Finally, the change agent needs to develop various techniques for determining both status level and the full complement of expectations both for himself and for everyone with whom he associates. He can afford to err early in the game, for there is a period of tolerance of his lack of knowledge and ability that lasts for about two years. From that time on, he is expected to know what status is about and what Latin society is all about. His mistakes will not be too well received and each one will be part of the increasing evidence for his own lowering status level. With each loss in standing, his influence declines until he is left in that very odd position of being unable to influence anyone. At that time it is wise for the change agent to close the books on that effort and withdraw.

The North American resists entering and mastering such a system since it is not only the opposite of his own, but he sees it as the opposite of what any thinking, logical person would want for himself. He thus needs to ask himself continually what is his purpose in entering Latin America. Does he wish to call attention to himself? Does he wish to call attention to his lifestyle, dress, organization, or decision making? Or, does he wish to influence the Latin for some purpose? If the latter is the case, there is nothing else to do but to pay attention to status, to extended family operations and to the patterns of reciprocity.

## Getting into family

The person who is in family either by blood or marrige rights or as if he were family through ritual ties is somebody. All others may be warm bodies, but they are in effect nobodies. The change agent needs to become part of a family. There is no guarantee that he will ever be invited into any given family. Therefore he needs to begin associating, when opportunity arises, with a number of extended families, primarily through one nuclear family within the whole. This can be done by being friendly, by opening up the process of reciprocity or by responding when a Latin has opened it, by making it a point to get to know heads of extended families and making positive steps toward acceptance into family. When children are announced or a wedding is being planned the change agent can show natural curiosity in the event. When the opportunity is extended for him to become a godparent or a coparent at birth or at marriage, he needs to cover himself by making clear the terms of the contract. Then once it is clear just what his responsibilities are, he can proceed to fulfill them with confidence.

Once a person becomes related to more than one extended family, care should be taken not to force them into association. He can enter one and leave it before he enters another in the ongoing affairs of life. It doesn't matter how many families a person is a ritual relative in. As long as he does not force the association of any two, he can be trusted and can proceed to accomplish his purposes.

## Providing the event

No association is fully validated in Latin society unless the association becomes meaningful through shared participation in experiences and events. These cannot be staged for the Latin—they need to bring him in through vital and integral participation. This means bringing him in at every stage of development. He must be part of its conceptualization, its planning and organization and its fulfillment. It must be that which draws positive response from him.

The means of embellishing the event must be carefully attended to. Within subcultures where tactile behavior is potential for embellishment, the agent of change needs to search out those aspects of tactile behavior that are proper and both stress and practice those. The *abrazo* is the hug of greeting and is lightly staged when people are strangers and becomes more like a bear hug for those who are close and intimate. The *abrazo* embellishes the event because it gives participants in an experience the feeling that it has begun well.

Great care needs to attend the list of participants in any event. The wrong people can quickly and effectively spoil the event. However much a change agent might want a given person at an event, if that person is potentially disruptive to the event it would be better to wait and bring him into association with the people another time and in another way.

## Relating to woman

No project or plan presented in Latin American is likely to reach its maximum peak of fulfillment unless the woman is an integral part of the plan. The woman must be there actually or ideologically. The conception of the woman and her place must fit into the various spots provided for her. This in no way means one's efforts are limited to the present level and development of Latin society and to woman's present place within society. Rather, it suggests that if woman is part of a plan, the plan has some hope of success, otherwise not.

The woman can be educator so long as she is working under higher status men. She can be the most effective intermediary in a majority of situations calling for one. She can be the vital link between God and man; for the Catholic as Mary the effective intermediary and for the Protestant as recognized mother of Jesus, good woman, model for women everywhere; one intermediary as intermediary type more than as sole mediator. The woman sets up the target so that it is placed well, is well lighted or highlighted, and is defined in relation to non-targets. With the woman part of the team, there is no end to what can be accomplished.

## Orienting the agent

The agent of change needs careful orientation to the various aspects of Latin life, especially those that are distinct from his own and call for automatic responses that hold different meanings than his own. The hug has a sexual connotation in many subcultures of North America. It triggers the wrong responses unless care is taken to divorce the hug from these connotations. Linguistic cues signal meanings opposite from that intended. To say "it lost itself" is like trying to get out of a nasty situation, and is therefore not manly to the North American. The hand movement of fingers extended downward which to the Latin signifies "come here" communicates the opposite to the North American. Drills need to be developed and participated in until the desired automatic response to the Latin cue is in keeping with the intent of the cue. It is not enough to have the drills of speech provided for by the Berlitz method of teaching Spanish. It is also important to have drills to shift one to the automatic responses of body movement and nonverbal cultural cues to behavior.

Simulations need to be developed or carried out that provide time on the driving machine, so to speak, before taking the car out on the road. Role playing actual situations that might arise from status, family, or reciprocity considerations pretune the person to the kinds of actual situations he is likely to meet when he enters a given subculture of Latin America. Systems games, being developed to teach American social structure, need to be developed to teach Latin social structure.

Finally, relationships can be developed wherever the change agent is in training that can prepare for the encounter to come. Both Latins and Latin-like people are near every training center. Effective relationships here help develop effective relationships there.

## For further reading

Huxley, Matthew, *Farewell to Eden,* Harper and Row, 1964.
Read, William R., Victor M. Monterroso and Harmon A. Johnson, *Latin American Church Growth,* Grand Rapids, Michigan, William B. Eerdmans Publishing Co., 1969.

# Bibliography

For each country of Latin America there are books, pamphlets and articles available for more specific application of the principles presented here. Such material is rich in valuable insight and should not be ignored.

Arciniegas, German, *The State of Latin America,* A. A. Knopf, N.Y., 1944.

Beyer, Glenn H., *The Urban Explosion in Latin America,* Cornell University Press, Ithaca, 1967.

Blasier, Cole, ed., *Constructive Change in Latin America,* University of Pittsburgh Press, 1968.

Cal, Tomme Clark, *The Mexican Venture,* Oxford University Press, 1953.

Freeman, Susan Tax, *Neighbors, The Social Contract in a Castilian Hamlet,* The University of Chicago Press, Chicago, 1971.

Fromm, Eric and Michael Maccoby, *Social Character in a Mexican Village, A Sociopsychoanalytic Study,* Prentice Hall, Englewood Cliffs, N.J., 1970.

Furtado, Celso, *Obstacles to Development in Latin America,* Doubleday and Co., Inc., Garden City, N.Y., 1970.

Gott, Richard, *Guerrilla Movements in Latin America,* Doubleday and Co., Garden City, N.Y., 1971.

Inman, Samuel G., *Latin America, Its Place in the World,* Willet, Clark and Co., 1937.

Moreno, Francisco Jose, *Legitimacy and Stability in Latin America, a Study of Chilean Political Culture,* New York University Press, N.Y., 1969.

Nehemkis, Peter, *Latin America, Myth and Reality,* Alfred A. Knopf, N.Y., 1964.

## Bibliography

O'Connor, Harvey, et al, *Whither Latin America,* Monthly Review Press, N.Y., 1963.

Peattie, Lisa Redfield, *The View from the Barrio,* Ann Arbor, The University Press, 1968.

Person, Donald, *Cruz Das Almas, A Brazilian Village,* Smithsonian Institution, Institute of Social Anthropology Publication 12, 1951.

Soule, George, et al, *Latin America in the Future of the World,* Farrar and Rinehart, 1945.

Steward, Julian H., et al, *The People of Puerto Rico,* University of Illinois Press, Urbana, 1956.

Tax, Sol, *Heritage of Conquest,* Free Press, Glencoe, Ill., 1952.

Terry, Robert H., *Comparative Readings on Latin America,* McCutchan Publishing Corp., Berkeley, Calif. 1969.